Bewitched

Walter Metz

TV MILESTONES SERIES

Wayne State University Press **Detroit**

© 2007 by Wayne State University Press,
Detroit, Michigan 48201. All rights reserved.
No part of this book may be reproduced without formal permission.
Manufactured in the United States of America.
11 10 09 08 07   5 4 3 2 1

Library of Congress Cataloging-in-Publication Data

Metz, Walter, 1967–
Bewitched / Walter Metz.
p. cm. — (TV milestones)
Includes bibliographical references.
ISBN-13: 978-0-8143-3231-3 (pbk. : alk. paper)
ISBN-10: 0-8143-3231-5 (pbk. : alk. paper)
1. Bewitched (Television program)   I. Title.
PN1992.77.B48M48 2007
791.45'72—dc22
2006031685

∞ The paper used in this publication meets the minimum requirements
of the American National Standard for Information Sciences—Permanence of Paper
for Printed Library Materials, ANSI Z39.48-1984.

Bewitched

TV Milestones

Series Editors

Barry Keith Grant
Brock University

Jeanette Sloniowski
Brock University

TV Milestones is part of the Contemporary Approaches to Film and Television Series

A complete listing of the books in this series can be found online at *http://wsupress.wayne.edu*

General Editor

Barry Keith Grant
Brock University

Advisory Editors

Patricia B. Erens
Dominican University

Robert J. Burgoyne
Wayne State University

Lucy Fischer
University of Pittsburgh

Tom Gunning
University of Chicago

Peter Lehman
Arizona State University

Anna McCarthy
New York University

Caren J. Deming
University of Arizona

Peter X. Feng
University of Delaware

CONTENTS

ACKNOWLEDGMENTS

As usual, I owe a tremendous debt to Anneke Metz. She inspired this book from beginning to end, watching *Bewitched* episodes with me, talking through ideas, and helping me to edit my often ungainly prose.

I also owe a great deal to the professors at the Department of Radio-Television-Film at the University of Texas at Austin, particularly Horace Newcomb, Thomas Schatz, and Janet Staiger. I came of age as an academic scholar under their excellent tutelage; particularly pertinent here is their resolve to teach critical and cultural studies to their graduate students in an environment that equally nurtures film and television scholarship. Now ten years past my doctoral work, I can fully appreciate how pertinent this is in contemporary media studies.

Were it not for a generous scholarship and creativity grant from Thomas McCoy, the vice president for research at Montana State University–Bozeman, I would not have been able to complete this work; I thank the administrators at MSU for having the courage to support humanities scholarship with an impressive array of resources given to non-science faculty such as myself.

Along the way, I received generous feedback on various drafts of the manuscript from Amanda Lotz and Diane Negra; I thank them for their insightful and careful readings.

My students at the University of Texas at Austin, Montana State University–Bozeman, and the John F. Kennedy Institute for North American Studies at the Free University Berlin have all had to endure many classes on the 1960s telefilm sitcom. I am proud to have finally finished the book to which they contributed through their patience, thoughtful insights, and many hours of discussion.

I also thank the excellent readers and staff at Wayne State University Press, particularly Annie Martin, the acquisitions editor, who was kind and patient during the inevitable delays in revision when one works as a writer and as a university teacher and administrator.

Introduction:
A Queer Children's Show

When I was eight years old in 1975, I would wake up and eat a bowl of cereal while watching *Bewitched* at 7:30 on a Boston UHF affiliate before setting off to school. Then, after school, I would run home at 3:30 and do my homework while again watching the show and its 1960s telefilm sitcom relatives—*Gilligan's Island* (CBS, 1964–67), *Get Smart* (NBC, 1965–69; CBS, 1969–70), *F-Troop* (ABC, 1965–67)—until 6:00 when my parents arrived home from work. Many of the textual features of *Bewitched,* originally broadcast on ABC in prime time, support the decision by local affiliates to air the show in syndication at times when primarily children would be watching.

Bewitched (ABC, 1964–72) concerns a witch, Samantha (Elizabeth Montgomery), her mortal husband, Darrin Stephens (Dick York in seasons 1–5, then Dick Sargent in seasons 6–8), and the troubles caused by this "mixed marriage." Samantha's witch identity represents a threat to Darrin's patriarchal head of household status and to his career as an advertising executive working under the amiable yet greedy Larry Tate (David White). Although the kinds of stories told in *Bewitched* are numerous and varied, the central conflict of the show shifts as the series develops.

In its first season, *Bewitched* emphasizes the odd newlyweds who desire an ordinary suburban life, but whose marital bliss is constantly threatened by the possibility that their secret might be discovered. This threat is most clearly articulated by the character of Gladys Kravitz (Alice Pearce in seasons 1–3, then Sandra Gould in seasons 3–8), the snooping neighbor. In its later seasons, the show maintains Darrin's attempt to enforce a mortal household as the central conflict, but shifts the threat from outside surveillance to the threat of family interference in the form of a never-ending stream of visits and meddling from Samantha's magical relatives. At first, Samantha's mother, Endora (Agnes Moorehead), and Uncle Arthur (Paul Lynde) cause most of the mischief, but later her father, Maurice (Maurice Evans), her look-alike cousin Serena (Elizabeth Montgomery again), and the witch maid Esmeralda (Alice Ghostley), among others, wreak havoc in Samantha and Darrin's domestic (and Darrin's professional) lives. My method in this book engages both of these textual systems, and more, rather than reducing the show to one overly general description that attempts to capture the essence of every episode. Whereas most other studies of this sitcom have analyzed at most a handful of episodes, I will explore the way in which the show looks very different depending upon which episodes are being considered. The interlocking textual systems of the *Bewitched* series that I will discuss include the identity politics of the Stephenses' unique marriage, the significance of history raised by characters popping into and out of the past, the cold war surveillance culture engaged by the fear of discovery of Samantha's secret, and the show's self-reflexive stance toward television itself.

The innovation in *Bewitched* criticism that I will attempt to make in this book emphasizes the episodes of the show in which characters from the past are brought into the present and, conversely, in which characters from the present return to the past. *Bewitched* takes a quite literal approach to representing the significance of the past to the present, and the politics of the present to the past. The book will apply Horace Newcomb's model of cumulative narrative to *Be-*

witched, moving beyond a film-based model of television textuality while at the same time demonstrating that this model is not limited to recent texts but even applies to "traditional" ones, such as 1960s telefilm sitcoms.

I will thus pursue a typology of *Bewitched,* not a reduction to the show's most representative or typical episode. This means, of course, that I have seen all of the episodes of *Bewitched* (some of them many times). While the notion of analyzing 127 hours of *Bewitched* could be construed as crazily excessive, a similar amount of time might be needed to analyze, for example, Marcel Proust's *Remembrance of Things Past.* Given that many literature scholars in fact make a career out of analyzing such a single, highly complex text, the time spent examining the entire run of *Bewitched* episodes seems a small investment, especially because the show is so rich in detail about 1960s and 1970s American television and culture. Such a statement about the importance of this "escapist fantasy" sitcom might incur more than just a little skepticism, especially since work on televisual textuality has largely failed to capture the scholarly imagination. However, it is my sincere hope that I will be able to erase some of the academic reservations regarding televisual scholarship and concurrently share with readers the joy of discovering so much about ourselves in this outwardly simple yet deeply complex slice of the American experience.

Many of the 254 episodes of *Bewitched*—which by its second season (1965–66) had, as *I Love Lucy* before it, morphed from a show about a young woman's struggles to support the public career of her newlywed husband into a domestic family sitcom about home life with children—feature literal fairy-tale narratives. For example, in episode #62 ("Baby's First Paragraph," 3/10/66), Endora tells the Stephenses' daughter, Tabitha, the "real" story of "Hansel and Gretel" because she cannot abide the negative stereotypes the Brothers Grimm forward about witches.[1] Similarly, in "A

Prince of a Guy" (#129, 2/8/68), Tabitha, also a witch, brings Prince Charming to life. When Larry Tate sees the man, whom he mistakes for an actor, he presses the storybook character into service as a corporate spokesman. The season premiere of the show's sixth season positions Tabitha and Samantha as the protagonists in a version of "Jack and the Beanstalk" (#171, "Samantha and the Beanstalk," 9/19/69). Incidentally, this is also the plot of an episode of *Gilligan's Island* (#66, "'V' for Vitamins," 4/14/66), in which Gilligan (Bob Denver) dreams he is Jack to the Skipper's beanstalk Giant (Alan Hale Jr.).

Because of this parade of assorted magical characters, animals, and the special effects associated with the portrayal of witchcraft, *Bewitched* appeals to children in a way that other more celebrated American sitcoms, such as *All in the Family* (CBS, 1971–83), never have. *All in the Family,* of course, was not directed toward children viewers, which is precisely the point; when CBS canceled its barnyard sitcoms and the like in the early 1970s, prime-time television changed dramatically. The telefilm sitcom of the 1960s operated under an industrial model that sought high ratings without much concern for demographics. When CBS executive Robert Wood replaced long-time populist programmer Mike Dann with Fred Silverman, the result was that networks sought "quality demographics" (audience members willing and able to spend on advertised products). CBS canceled many of its popular shows, which appealed to rural, young and older viewers, and replaced them with fare deemed more socially relevant, like *All in the Family.*[2] Such industrial pressures in the early 1970s no doubt entered into ABC's decision to cancel *Bewitched* in 1972, although Elizabeth Montgomery's desire to do other projects certainly was another major factor.

This much is common knowledge in television history. What remains is a need to study the adult/child crossover ap-

peal typical of the 1960s sitcom, both textually and industri-
ally—not to reveal these shows' juvenile content, but to better understand the complexity of shows that could appeal to
both adults and children. In her feminist essay on what she
calls the "fantastic family sit-com," Lynn Spigel produces an
implicit call to attend to the demographics of *Bewitched*'s audience: "It is important to keep in mind that the genre at-
tracted many child viewers who would have had a limited
knowledge of the classic family sit-com as well as different
social/historical backgrounds from adults in the audience"
(234–35). I want to begin by framing my current, academic
interest in *Bewitched* through the reason I am so familiar and
fascinated by the show—namely, my status as an obsessive,
childhood fan. This tension is not only crucial for considering what kind of television critics academics are, but in the
case of *Bewitched*, also helps address its seemingly contradictory status as an important adult show about feminism and a
reviled children's show about witches and warlocks. *TV
Guide* critic Ronald Searle is one of many *Bewitched* detractors: "I know that the canned laughter underscoring those
mournful lines in *Bewitched* is the laughter of lost souls. . . .
Who else would applaud so hysterically the words: 'What's
for breakfast, Sam?' They know what's for breakfast. We are,
sunny side up" (18).

The two children in my family span the baby-boomer
generation: my brother was born in 1949 to a young postwar
mother; I came eighteen years later, in 1967. While my
brother grew up on foundational 1950s television—he talks
a lot about his pride in his Davy Crockett hat—I grew up on
1970s nostalgia television such as *Happy Days* (ABC,
1974–84) and recycled fantasy sitcoms from the 1960s. To
the child that I was in the 1970s, along with most of my late
baby-boomer peers, *Bewitched* was a cute children's show
about fairy tales and good witches. While studying media
history in graduate school, I discovered a significantly more

adult *Bewitched,* a show largely about women's liberation. It quickly became clear to me that prime-time television of the 1960s is not just the childish delight I had assumed it to be. Instead, *Bewitched* also turns out to be an adult delight, engaging in a strong-willed critique of discrimination of those who cannot or will not abide by conventional social mores.

The opening lines of the pilot, "I, Darrin, Take This Witch, Samantha" (9/17/64), are spoken by a voice-over narrator (an uncredited José Ferrer) introducing us to the courtship of Samantha and Darrin as a fairy tale, but significantly, one for adults: "Once upon a time, there was a typical American girl who happened to bump into a typical American boy." The narrator tells us that Sam and Darrin have a lot in common; the joke is of images showing the two lovers kissing all around town, incessantly. The pilot's comic concern with a sociological fairy tale about the courtship rituals of young adults in early 1960s America is far from the cute representations of literal fairy tales in the episodes to come.

Nothing establishes the adult sensibility of *Bewitched* more than its queer theoretical subtext. The show, it turns out, was populated with the major figures of popular gay American culture of the 1960s. The analysis of these figures has concentrated on Agnes Moorehead, the flamboyant matriarch of the show, and Paul Lynde, who played Arthur, Samantha's gay (in both the naïve and cosmopolitan sense), wise-cracking, beloved uncle. The second actor to play Darrin, Dick Sargent, while closeted at the time of the show, outed himself in the late 1980s. In retrospect, it is clear that Sargent played the role of Darrin, the "normal" husband and father on *Bewitched,* with an angry, sardonic edge not brought to the role by his predecessor Dick York, who offered a more genial, beleaguered interpretation.

In the best study of *Bewitched* as a queer text, Patricia White assesses the film and television work of Mercedes McCambridge, who guest starred in episode #144 ("Darrin Gone

Sam and Darrin's first meeting, in "I, Darrin, Take This Witch, Samantha" (9/17/64).

and Forgotten," 10/17/68) as Carlotta, a witch who imprisons Darrin because years before Endora promised her that Samantha would marry her effeminate son, Juke. Sam spends the episode teaching Juke to become a man and stand up to his overbearing mother. At the end, he does, and Sam's marriage to Darrin is saved yet again. White links McCambridge's performance of Carlotta to McCambridge's star persona, both from films such as *Johnny Guitar* (Nicholas Ray, 1953)—"Her black-clad villain in this dyke western makes her co-star Joan Crawford look femme as she wreaks twisted vengeance and dies the requisite homo-death" (178)—and to other guest appearances on 1960s fantasy television shows: "She is memorable as the woman who wanted to marry television's perhaps most memorable villainous/scapegoat/camp queer, Dr. Smith on *Lost in Space*" (179).

White states that *Bewitched*'s credentials as a queer cultural artifact are extensive, from its thematic obsessions to its large list of gay/lesbian actors: "Darrin's anxiety about his wife's powers are well-founded: she belongs to a matriarchal order of superior beings" (192). However, the specific case of Agnes Moorehead is what most interests White in her pursuit of the popular representation of lesbian identity in American culture. White quotes an interview with Paul Lynde in which he says, "Well, the whole world knows Agnes was a lesbian— I mean classy as hell, but one of the all-time Hollywood dykes" (qtd. in White, 140). This came as quite a surprise to me: Herbie Pilato's fan book about *Bewitched* emphasizes Moorehead's Christian Fundamentalism, citing a work called *Good Dames* by James Robert Parish in which Moorehead is quoted as saying, "My life has been ruled by my beliefs ('working for the glory of God') and in matters of belief I am a Fundamentalist" (qtd. in Pilato, 24–25). Pilato never mentions any suspicion that Moorehead may have been a closeted lesbian. Yet whether Agnes Moorehead—a wonderful character actress famous for her work in Orson Welles's *Citizen Kane* (1941) and Douglas Sirk's *All That Heaven Allows* (1955)— was actually a lesbian or not misses the point. White explains: "Regardless of whether the lady really was a lesbian, the characterization complements her persona. It is no mere queer coincidence that Agnes Moorehead can be dubbed one of the all-time Hollywood supporting actresses and one of the all-time Hollywood dykes" (140). This observation forms the thesis of White's book: many great Hollywood character actresses resonate with lesbian identity—either literally or allegorically—because of the marginalization of lesbianism in homophobic U.S. culture. Sidekicks and marginal villains become the ideal places for Hollywood to house its literal and symbolic lesbians.

The queer reading of *Bewitched* is not confined to Patricia White's analysis of lesbian identity. Paul Lynde as Uncle

Arthur has in fact become the central reference for a campy understanding of queer culture on American television. In a skillful reading of Todd Haynes's queer reconstruction of the films of Douglas Sirk, *Far from Heaven* (2002), Sharon Willis uses Lynde as a cultural benchmark to explain the behavior of the film's central male protagonist, Frank Whitaker (Dennis Quaid), a family man who discovers that he is gay:

> Frank erupts with the hysterical force we might have expected from Kyle Hadley in *Written on the Wind*. Contouring his body back onto the couch, and affecting a tone lifted directly from Paul Lynde, arguably TV's favorite unacknowledged queer of the 1970s, Frank blurts out: "It's all smoke an mirrors, fellas." Wrinkling his nose and baring his teeth in a signature Lynde grimace while allowing his hands to hang limp in an additional flourish as his body convulses in disgust, he delivers this blow: "You should see [Cathy, his wife] before she puts her face on." (146)

In short, queer criticism restructures *Bewitched* as a quintessentially adult television show, a forerunner to another, more controversial late 1970s ABC sitcom, *Soap* (1977–81), which featured a gay male character, Jodie (Billy Crystal). Jodie would go on to "explore" heterosexuality, fathering a baby and fighting its mother for custody. No such equivocation characterizes Uncle Arthur: he camped around Samantha's house from his first appearance (#41, "The Joker Is a Card," 10/14/65) to his last (#218, "The House That Uncle Arthur Built," 2/11/71).

Even *before* playing Uncle Arthur, Lynde camped it up on *Bewitched*: in episode #26 ("Driving Is the Only Way to Fly," 3/25/65), he played Harold, Sam's driving instructor. In its positioning of Harold's masculinity as out of sync with 1960s America, the episode is overdetermined. It begins with

Darrin trying to watch baseball on television. Sam, however, wants the driving lesson Darrin has promised her; she typically relies on flying as her mode of transportation, a behavior with which Darrin passionately disagrees. When Sam again defends the benefits of her way, Darrin as usual invokes his sense of normalcy, claiming that the baseball game she is distracting him from, as well as driving, are both "part of the American Dream." Sam slyly interferes with the baseball part of Americana so that she can partake of the car culture, casting a spell behind Darrin's back that makes it rain at the ballpark, forcing the umpires to postpone the game.

When Darrin proves too sexist to actually instruct Sam in how to drive—he unctuously says that women's driving gestures typically involve blowing on one's fingernails to dry polish!—he makes an appointment for her with the Reliable Driving School. There, a different, yet no more problematic, form of normative masculinity, the gruff working-class owner, Basil, assigns Harold to Sam's lesson, telling him aggressively that this is his one last chance. Harold, a nervous Nellie, is allowed to work for Basil only because he is his wife's errant brother. Harold, in fact, is such a deviant within this family that he has been fired from four other jobs, given to him by four other, presumably normal, brothers-in-law!

When Endora intervenes in the driving lesson, Harold runs away from the witchcraft, in hysterics. A Good Samaritan to the end, Sam insists that Harold run all of her driving lessons in the future, making it impossible for Basil to fire Harold. In the episode's coda, Harold visits Sam and Darrin at their home. Sam has transformed him into a confident, socially functional young man. He is still as queer as ever, though, now teaching basket weaving. The power of Sam's socially constructive deviance results in the transformation of the world, as even annoyingly normal Darrin agrees to come to the class with Sam.

As Arthur, Paul Lynde (with a queer force not matched

on American television until John Waters crashed the Simpsons' household nearly thirty years later ["Homer's Phobia," 2/16/97]) personified the queer uncle crashing the normative middle-class American home to bathe it in camp. Arthur's delight in playing practical jokes on Darrin, coupled with his genuine love for Sam, caused playful chaos to reign in the Stephenses' household. His queer character is also a key link between the surface kiddie appeal of the show and its prime-time status as a show for adults.

The best example of the tension between childhood and adulthood in *Bewitched* is an Uncle Arthur episode in which the family celebrates Tabitha's birthday, "A Bunny for Tabitha" (#178, 11/6/69). Uncle Arthur mistakenly conjures up a Playboy Bunny during a magic show at Tabitha's birthday party. The twist is that "Bunny" has not simply been zapped over from one of Hugh Hefner's men's clubs popular at the time. She is in fact a real rabbit, transformed into human form by Uncle Arthur's wayward spell. A visiting client promptly falls in love with the dimwitted blonde vegetarian, and the dialogue quickly becomes loaded with sexual innuendo, with lots of jokes about rabbits "doing what they do best." The scene makes fun of the stereotypical image of the airhead beauty (in this case she is so stupid because she really is a rabbit), but simultaneously pokes fun at the man who does his thinking below the belt. The client and the bunny leave together shortly after they meet, resulting in the episode's equating men's behavior with the infamously procreative behavior of rabbits. The force of Paul Lynde's camp performance style (foppish, irreverent, sarcastic) queers the episode's notions of normal (that is to say, exploitative!) notions of male sexual predation. In the world of Uncle Arthur, men wanting to have sex with Playboy Bunnies is not celebrated, it is literally zoocrastia.

Sam and Darrin forestall a disastrous quickie marriage by getting the ill-matched couple to recognize their differ-

Queer Uncle Arthur (Paul Lynde) is perplexed by a Playboy Bunny, in "A Bunny for Tabitha" (11/6/69).

12

ences: she wants "lots and lots" of children, while he likes to hunt rabbits! In the end, Uncle Arthur's spell to return the bunny to her original animal state misfires and produces a chorus line of six (confused with "sex" in Arthur's misspeaking of the spell) identical Playboy Bunnies all lined up in the Stephenses' back yard. Sam, as usual, straightens things out, but Arthur will be back to camp another day.

While ABC's airing of *Soap* was picketed by religious groups and caused a tremendous cultural ado—Tim Brooks and Earle Marsh report that ABC received nine letters in support and 32,000 against (952)—*Bewitched* was broadcast without incident, and in fact became a morning and afternoon syndication ritual for a whole generation of children such as myself. And so the question becomes: which reading—a kiddie show or an adult allegory—is correct? Both readings are defensible. *Bewitched* is a polysemous show, constituted by narrative complexity and contradiction. Indeed, this neglected historical moment in television history—the 1960s with its fantasy and barnyard situation comedies—may be television's most fertile site for performing ideological analysis of the medium's ability to engage in social critique. The joys, childish or otherwise, of *Bewitched* can only be enhanced by appreciating the show's hitherto neglected complexity.

A long-running television series can indeed develop complexity precisely because it consists of such a large number of episodes delivered over a time span of many years. This is even more so since such shows are penned by a cast of multiple and changing writers, and reflect different sensibilities and changing public interests over the passage of time. This complexity of the televisual narrative calls for new techniques to assess the full scope of the medium's textual meaning. One method for visualizing the complexity of series television is to reformulate the appropriate scope for the analysis of the television text, considering the text of a show to be not a representative episode or two, but its entire run, thoroughly accounted for with detailed analysis tracking shifts and nuances in its modulation of aesthetic style, narrative structure, and ideological position.

An Industrial History of *Bewitched*

Bewitched, through its 254 half-hour episodes, both participated in industrial innovations—the conversion from black-and-white to color television, for example—and witnessed the political shift from Lyndon Johnson's Great Society to Richard Nixon's particular brand of conservatism. In fact, in a perfect instance of the historical uncanny, the creative team responsible for *Bewitched*—creator Sol Saks, executive producer Harry Ackerman, and director William Asher—began filming the pilot, about the occult destabilization of the conformist life of an upwardly mobile advertising man, on the very day in November 1963 when President Kennedy was assassinated. Asher and star Elizabeth Montgomery (who were married at the time) felt particularly close to Kennedy since Asher had produced the now infamous televised birthday party of President Kennedy in which Marilyn Monroe sang, "Happy birthday, Mr. President." Despite the deep-felt loss, the cast and crew showed up to the set to begin filming the pilot. As Asher noted in an interview with Herbie Pilato, "We knew we had to go on" (3). As it turned out, the production spanned the rest of the turbulent decade of the 1960s, witnessed the 1969 landing on the moon, and was still spinning its particular brand of magic as the Nixon administration began its second term. The show was canceled in the spring of 1972, airing its last episode, provocatively titled, given the importance of the impending Watergate scandal, "The Truth, Nothing but the Truth, So Help Me, Sam" on March 25, 1972.

ABC first broadcast *Bewitched* on September 17, 1964, and it enjoyed strong popularity for much of its eight-year run. The show was the network's longest-running and highest-rated sitcom during the years it was on the air. In its first season, it was ABC's number one show, and the number two show of the season among all three networks, running behind only NBC's western family drama *Bonanza* (1959–73), a remarkable feat considering ABC's reliance on its predominantly UHF stations with far less coverage than that of the other two major networks.

The All-Channel Receiver Law of 1962, which forced television-set manufacturers to include UHF reception capabilities on all of their products (including sets made by NBC's parent company RCA), compensated for ABC's affiliate-weakened position as *Bewitched* began airing. By the end of *Bewitched*'s run, ABC had fully recovered from its poor start in the industry and was primed to become the number one network. ABC became the ratings leader for the first time in its history in the mid- to late 1970s, in large part due to the success of *Happy Days* and *Laverne and Shirley* (1976–83), similarly preposterous sitcoms (although nostalgic rather than magical) about gender and history.

Bewitched premiered in the Thursday evening 9 p.m. time slot, serving as a remarkable bridge between the soft-hearted domestic family sitcom, *My Three Sons,* and the distinctly adult prime-time soap opera, *Peyton Place.* This placement is a clear indication of *Bewitched*'s crossover appeal between children and adult viewers, the contradiction with which I began, and which will continue to frame this study.[3] *My Three Sons,* the 13th highest-rated show that season, provided a relatively strong lead-in. With the 9th rated second installment of the prime-time soap *Peyton Place* immediately following (*Peyton Place* was shown Tuesday and Thursday nights from 9:30 to 10 p.m.), this three-series block was ABC's strongest ratings grabber of the 1964 season.[4]

Bewitched continued to be strong in the ratings for the next four seasons. It was the 7th highest rated show in both the 1965 and 1966 seasons, and the 11th highest rated show in both the 1967 and 1968 seasons. It also won three Emmys, one for William Asher (directing, 1966), and two posthumous awards for actresses Alice Pearce (in 1966 for her portrayal of nosy neighbor, Gladys Kravitz) and Marion Lorne (in 1968 for her work as the endearingly bumbling witch, Aunt Clara).

In its sixth season (1969), *Bewitched* dropped precipitously in the ratings to number 24. This was the first season in which Dick Sargent replaced Dick York as the actor portraying Darrin Stephens. It was also now running opposite stronger shows on the other networks. By now *Bewitched* was

15

showing on Thursday nights at 8:30 p.m. In this time slot, it had been up against NBC's crime drama *Ironside* (NBC, 1967–75) since 1967, but by now *Ironside* had successfully built an audience. The Raymond Burr detective show ranked 16th in 1968, moved up to 15th in 1969, and would become the 4th highest-ranked show on TV in 1970.

In addition, CBS had two top-25 shows in its 1969 Thursday night lineup, *Family Affair* (1966–71; 7:30–8 p.m., number 5) and *The Jim Nabors Hour* (1969–71; 8–9 p.m., number 12). By 1970, up against NBC's back-to-back showings of the 2nd ranked *The Flip Wilson Show* (1970–74; 7:30–8:30) and *Ironside* (8:30–9:30), *Bewitched* fell out of the top-25 altogether. In its final season, it was moved to Wednesday nights at 8 p.m., where it was unable to pull up in the ratings opposite CBS's innovative variety-comedy formatted *The Carol Burnett Show* (1967–79; number 25 for the season) and NBC's *Adam 12* (1968–75; number 8 for the season).

Bewitched was popular and original enough to prompt the creation of a rival show featuring a magical woman, NBC's *I Dream of Jeannie,* which appeared on the television schedule in 1965. Although it was broadcast for five years, until 1970, *Jeannie*'s ratings never rivaled *Bewitched,* and it never broke into the top-25. A second sitcom inspired by the original *Bewitched* proved even less popular. *Tabitha*, a 1977 ABC "spin-off" featuring the now twenty-something Stephens daughter (played by Lisa Hartman), never clicked with viewers, and did not survive the season. This may have been partially due to Tabitha's precocious maturity in the new show. As if a character on a soap opera, Tabitha was born on *Bewitched* in 1966 and only six when the show went off the air. Tabitha should have been eleven in 1977, an age that would not have worked with *The Mary Tyler Moore Show* (CBS, 1970–77) out-on-my-own—can she make it after all?— plotlines of the new show.

The success of *Bewitched* should be attributed to snappy writing, the charm of its series star, Elizabeth Montgomery, and the talent of its large supporting cast, which included such notable contemporary stars as Dick York, Agnes Moorehead, and Marion Lorne. In addition, the show offered remarkable aesthetic technique. Beyond the elegant film style with which the pilot was shot, the technical details of the show's delivery offer direct continuity with respected film techniques. To make characters disappear, the camera was stopped, the actor removed, and the filming resumed. This technique had been used in the cinema since Georges Méliès. The soundtrack was also unique, especially the synthesized sound that made Elizabeth Montgomery's nose twitch all that more special. Furthermore, the show's creators made the aesthetics of the show part of its thematic concerns. For example, the synchronization of sound with image is, in a modernist sense, interrogated in "Out of Sync, Out of Mind" (#116, 11/2/67), in which Aunt Clara accidentally casts a spell on Sam that causes her speech to be out of sync with the movement of her lips, a problem that causes Sam some difficulty since her in-laws happen to be visiting at the time.

While ratings indicate that the show waned in popularity in its later years, I suggest that some of the show's most vibrant material was produced late in its run. An industrial analysis is thus not the best tool for understanding the importance of episodes aired as the ratings waned. Instead, this book will explore the ideological meanings of the show, which become more intriguing as the writers were forced to produce innovations in the sitcom form (Sam and Darrin go to Salem and confront Puritan repression in a series of episodes that begin the seventh season) and to return to the sitcom's roots (the couple goes to Europe, as did Lucy and Ricky before them, in the set of episodes that begin the eighth and final season).

Contextualizing *Bewitched:* Witches, Film, and Television

Such a discussion of *Bewitched* in continuity with the history of television allows us to study how a mature form of comedy developed from one era to the next. *Bewitched,* after all, came out of distinct traditions, televisual certainly, but also filmic and more generally cultural. On this latter front, *Bewitched*'s position has much to do with the popular history of postwar American feminism. In February 1964, Betty Friedan, the by-then famous author of *The Feminine Mystique* (1963), published an application of her book's liberal feminist method to the history of television. The essay, "Television and the Feminine Mystique," lambasted American television's representation of women: "Television's image of the American woman, 1964, is a stupid, unattractive, insecure little household drudge who spends her martyred, mindless, boring days dreaming of love—and plotting nasty revenge against her husband" (93). Few moments in cultural history mark when a clarion call for social change has been met with the kind of force through which *Bewitched* responded to Friedan's critique.

Samantha on *Bewitched* represented an antidote to the kind of women Friedan lamented about being on American television; in fact, Endora uses Friedan's exact words, such as "drudge" and "boring," to describe Sam's life with Darrin. In her reflections on *Bewitched,* Susan Douglas studies an early episode of the series, "Eat at Mario's" (#35, 5/27/65), in which Sam and Endora befriend an Italian immigrant who refuses the commercialization of pizza, instead demanding that his customers eat his sophisticated continental cuisine. Endora particularly delights in defending Mario against the crass commercialism represented by Darrin, who is running the ad campaign for a rival Americanized pizza franchiser in town. Douglas analyzes a scene in which Endora and Saman-

Endora smokes opium in Sam's suburban home, in "Divided He Falls" (5/5/66).

tha (before she knows Mario's is in direct competition with one of Darrin's clients) use their witchcraft to ensure the Italian restaurant's success. Endora and Samantha revel in their transgressions. Douglas argues, "The delight they take in orchestrating this ad campaign is clear as each tackles a new medium, giggling and saying, 'It's your turn,' and 'Now, yours'" ("Genies and Witches" 130). In this way, Douglas delights in the women taking an active, aggressive role in the public space, the ideal antidote to the kinds of representations that angered Friedan.

Bewitched's place in cultural history can also be analyzed through its sophistication as a filmed representation of witches. Unlike other sitcoms of the era—*Gilligan's Island,* for example—*Bewitched* was written and filmed with the sophistication of Hollywood romantic comedies. The first episodes feature a voice-over narrator performing comic sociological analyses of Sam's role as a witch in middle-class suburbia, similar in tone to such 1950s film comedies as *Will*

Success Spoil Rock Hunter? (Frank Tashlin, 1958), a film critical of men's roles in advertising culture.

Two films about witches stand out as precursors to *Bewitched*'s genial representation of female witches: *I Married a Witch* (Rene Clair, 1942) and *Bell, Book and Candle* (Richard Quine, 1958). As a romantic comedy, *Bewitched* offers a textual synthesis of these two films, mixing the down-home Americana of Clair's film with the celebration of the modern urban style featured in Quine's. *Bewitched*, in all its textual complexity, can be read as an extended intertextual adaptation of these two films. Featuring an interest in the melodramatization of history that *Bewitched* would also pursue, *I Married a Witch* shows how romance can undo the historical sins of a culture. In the film, Fredric March plays Wallace Wooley, whose ancestors burned witches at Salem. As revenge, the witch victim, Jennifer (Veronica Lake), attempts to curse Jonathan with a love potion. Instead, screwball hilarity ensues, and *she* mistakenly takes the potion and falls in love with Wallace. This produces a love triangle complication, as Wallace is supposed to marry Estelle (Susan Hayward) in order to secure his political ambitions and allow him to run for public office.

From beginning to end, *I Married a Witch* produces a framework for fusing a romantic comedy about a witch falling in love with a mortal to a meditation on core American themes. As with a number of *Bewitched* episodes, the film begins in Puritan New England. The film jokes about witch burning as crass theater: a man sells goods to the crowd as Jennifer burns at the stake. In the *Bewitched* episode, "Paul Revere Rides Again" (#206, 10/29/70), the befuddled witch Esmeralda accidentally summons Paul Revere from the past. Only when Darrin convinces his client, Sir Leslie Bancroft, that the man is part of an advertising campaign is he able to extricate himself from trouble. In this way, both *I Married a Witch* and *Bewitched* construct a critique of capitalism as the glue that holds American culture together, ironically pinning these values to the nation's Puritan roots.

I Married a Witch builds its examination of present-day America via images that link Wallace Wooley to the U.S. past. For example, one of the film's running gags is Jennifer's assault on the pictures of Wooley's ancestors. When Jennifer first spends time in Wallace's apartment, she finds a portrait of Jonathan Wooley. Jennifer angrily waves her arm at the portrait, knocking it off the wall. Later in the film, as Jennifer gives Wallace the love potion that is to make him fall in love with her so that she can dominate him "like a slave," a 1904 photograph of one of Wooley's ancestors knocks Jennifer unconscious. Wallace offers the dazed Jennifer some of the potion to revive her, thinking it is water, setting up the love triangle that drives the plot of the film.

Bewitched similarly relies on portraits and photographs as markers of the past's impingement on the present. In the episode "Eye of the Beholder" (#22, 2/25/65), Sam, Darrin, and Endora browse in an antique shop. Once again angry that Sam is rejecting her witch heritage, Endora causes trouble by zapping Sam's visage into a painting, "The Maid of Salem" from 1682. Darrin spots the painting and, thinking that Sam really was a maid of Salem, buys it, hides it in his closet, and spirals into despair.

This precipitates one of the show's most touching love scenes. Recovering from a drinking binge, Darrin sits and sulks at the park. He overhears a conversation between an elderly couple about the day they first met. Sam pops in at the park to reconcile with Darrin. Before she can explain her mother's trickery, Darrin apologizes to Sam, "I love you, and that's all that matters." Still trying to cause trouble in the epilogue, Endora zaps a photo of a seventy-five-year-old Darrin into a picture frame on the stand next to Sam's bed. Sam merely twitches it back to a current photo of Darrin and the episode ends with true love triumphant.

21

I Married a Witch features a witch whose father is diabolically angry with mortals. In Clair's film, the devilish Daniel, Jennifer's father, plots with her to ruin the Wooley descendants. *Bewitched* features Maurice, Samantha's powerful warlock father who has no patience for mortals. In *I Married a Witch*, Daniel threatens to turn Wallace into a frog. Maurice similarly threatens Darrin in *Bewitched*. However, in both texts, the love between female witch and mortal man triumphs over such angry parental meddling. At the end of *I Married a Witch*, Jennifer tricks the besotted Daniel into vaporizing his essence into a bottle of whiskey. She corks the bottle, allowing her and Wallace to live happily ever after. The film's epilogue, announced by a title card reading "And the Future?" shows Wallace and Jennifer as the proud parents of witches as Daniel remains drunkenly locked in his bottle.

This blissful domestic ending of *I Married a Witch* is fully in keeping with the resolutions of *Bewitched,* at the level of the individual episodes and of the series as a whole. The epilogue to Clair's film is most similar to a dream sequence housed within the *Bewitched* episode titled ". . . And Something Makes Three" (#12, 12/3/1964). In this episode, Larry accidentally overhears Louise and Sam in an obstetrician's office. Larry mistakenly thinks Sam is pregnant, when in fact it is Louise who is with child. When Larry tells Darrin that he is going to be a father, he begins to worry about whether the child will be a witch or not. In his daydream reverie, Darrin imagines one day when Sam brings their kids to his office. Stereotypically dressed as witches with black hats and capes, they are ill-behaved hellions, running chaotically and unchecked over his office. One of the girls, little Endora (played by Maureen McCormick, soon to be Marsha on *The Brady Bunch*), changes her brother into a potted plant. While Darrin does not become a father that day, later in the show, Sam does end up having two children, Tabitha and Adam, both with magical powers. Despite Tabitha's uncontrolled

Darrin dreams he is the father of a brood of witches, in ". . . And Something Makes Three" (12/3/64).

use of her "wishcraft," Darrin lives with his family in domestic bliss, similar to the romantic comedy resolution of *I Married a Witch*.

The most direct influence of *I Married a Witch* on *Bewitched* can be found in the show's pilot episode. Two developments of the love triangle between mortal Wallace, his snobbish fiancée, Estelle, and Jennifer the witch are crucial for *Bewitched*. First, Daniel attempts to protect Jennifer from getting hurt: "Telling a mortal that you're a witch will only be the end of you." Second, Daniel uses magic to wreak havoc on the wedding guests. Daniel summons hurricane-force winds, ruining everyone's clothing, causing Estelle to sob, "My gown is ruined!" These two gestures describe the two major movements of the *Bewitched* pilot. In the first act, in the honeymoon suite, Endora tries to convince Sam not to marry the mortal Darrin. Undeterred, Sam convinces the unbelieving Darrin that she is really a witch, without scaring him off. Then, in the second act, Darrin's ex-girlfriend Sheila Summers holds a swank dinner party for the sole purpose of humiliating Samantha. When Sam has finally had enough, she uses her magic to unzip Sheila's dress and summons gale-force winds that fling Sheila's wig off of her head, giving the snobbish debutante the comeuppance she deserves.

Bell, Book and Candle similarly utilizes this love triangle plot. Shep Henderson (James Stewart) is about to marry Merle Kittridge (Janice Rule), an old college rival of his beautiful neighbor, Manhattanite Gillian Holroyd (Kim Novak), a witch. Like Jennifer before her, Gillian casts a spell on Shep in an attempt to have a meaningless fling, but when she really falls in love with him, romantic comedy mayhem ensues. If *Bewitched* inherits from *I Married a Witch* an emphasis on the historical effects of Puritanism on contemporary American marriage rituals, then from *Bell, Book and Candle* it receives an infusion of "hip." *Bell, Book and Candle* represents an elegant examination of witchcraft as urban transgression; it forwards a contrast between the sophisticated witches, associated with the Zodiac Club, a Greenwich Village beatnik hangout in which Gillian's brother, Nicky (Jack Lemmon), is a bongo drummer and a warlock. In *Bewitched,* the parallel character is Serena, Samantha's alter ego cousin, who loves the hippie lifestyle and, like Endora, belittles Darrin's world as "a quarter acre of crabgrass" (#2, "Be It Ever So Mortgaged," 9/24/64).

As a sitcom, the major context for understanding *Bewitched* is its location in the history of television. *Bewitched* frequently announced its relationship to the history of television comedy. For example, Imogene Coca from *Your Show of Shows* guest starred as the tooth fairy in a two-part story—"Mary the Good Fairy" and "The Tooth Fairy Strikes Again" (#215 and #216, 1/21 and 1/28/71)—in which she uses her considerable comic skills to embody the magical lady with a drinking problem. One night, Mary the fairy comes to take

Tabitha's tooth, but stays for a shot of brandy, awakening Darrin and Sam. Unfamiliar with such mortal spirits, Mary gets "crocked" (as Samantha puts it), forcing Sam to take over her rounds that night. When Mary continues her drinking binge, Sam is stuck with the fairy wings. Sam notes to nosy neighbor Mrs. Kravitz, who unwittingly gives Mary more brandy after Darrin locks the Stephenses' liquor cabinet, that "aunt" Mary "has a little problem." This fairy-tale story again demonstrates the slick way in which *Bewitched* is able to spread its appeal to both adults and children, slipping in jokes about alcoholism while delighting the younger set with a fairy tale come-to-life.

One further example of *Bewitched*'s resonance with earlier television is evident in a comparison to *The Goldbergs* (CBS, 1949–51; NBC, 1952–53; DUM, 1954; first-run syndication, 1955–56), a 1950s sitcom about a Jewish immigrant family trying to achieve the American dream. While George Lipsitz suggests that the early 1950s ethnic sitcom was banished from the airwaves by a middle-class takeover of American television (103), it is possible to see *Bewitched* as a continuation of the ethnic sitcom in allegorical form. In an episode from the 1955–56 season, which ran in first-run syndication, the Goldberg family agonizes over providing their daughter, Rosalie, with singing lessons that they cannot afford when they mistakenly believe that she has professional vocal talent.

During the course of the episode, titled "The Singer," the family decides that any sacrifice is worth the possibility of enabling the children to assimilate. The show ends happily when the singing teacher tells the family truthfully that the daughter does not really have the talent to be a professional after all. The pressure is thus taken off Rosalie, who did not really want to pursue a singing career and who knew the lessons were too expensive, but who also did not want to disappoint her proud parents. This contrasts well with the "Samantha at the Keyboard" episode of *Bewitched* (#143, 10/10/68), in which Sam and Darrin protect Tabitha from a career as a (magical) piano prodigy, finding a hungry talent agent (played by Jonathan Harris, the campy Dr. Smith from *Lost in Space*) a "real" prodigy, the son of a poor black school janitor, instead. Sam and Darrin protect their daughter from the rigors of a public life, and also forward a patronizing agenda of the white protector and promoter of poor African Americans. Consistent with its ethnic sitcom roots, *Bewitched* finds a way to make assimilation the main theme of the episode, even if such assimilation does not concern their own daughter, as it did for the Goldbergs.

Far and away the most obvious and important connection between *Bewitched* and the history of television is the huge debt the show owes to *I Love Lucy* (CBS, 1951–61). The basic premise of *Bewitched,* that of a woman relegated to the private space by her patriarchal husband only to threaten in every episode to burst into public visibility, continues until 1972, with nary one season's gap, the basic premise of *I Love Lucy* begun in 1951. There was indeed a creative bridge between the sensibility of the two shows via *Bewitched*'s executive producer and consultant, Harry Ackerman, who served as vice-president for CBS programming in Hollywood during the *I Love Lucy* years. Ackerman worked together with Lucille Ball, Desi Arnaz, and Jess Oppenheimer to develop the *I Love Lucy* concept, and also personally supervised its production (Pilato 297).

I Love Lucy and *Bewitched* also share a common family trajectory. *I Love Lucy* started out as a show about Lucy and Ricky, and only later involved their child, little Ricky, who was born on the show. Similarly, Sam and Darrin's first child, Tabitha, was not born until the second season, and was not seen regularly until several years after that. Thus, unlike most family sitcoms that revolve around the lives of already established families—*Father Knows Best* (CBS, 1954–55 and

1958–62; NBC, 1955–58; ABC, 1962–63) and *My Three Sons* (ABC, 1960–65; CBS, 1965–72) in that period, and *The Simpsons* (FOX, 1989–present) in ours—both of these shows dealt with the pregnancies of the show's main characters and the birth of their children. *I Love Lucy* was a trailblazing show in this regard, being the first to even deal with pregnancy, a subject previously considered too indecent for television. Even on *I Love Lucy*, the show that broke the news of Lucy's pregnancy had to be titled "Lucy Is *Enciente*" (#50, 12/8/52) to bypass network censors (being French and pregnant, is, apparently, acceptable!).

Samantha had two pregnancies during the run of *Bewitched*, for daughter Tabitha ("born" on 1/13/66) and son Adam ("born" during season 6, on 10/16/69). By the time Samantha got pregnant, it was not a problem to mention "pregnancy" on television, and indeed the word is used liberally in the "Divided He Falls" episode (#69, 5/5/66), later remade as "Samantha's Better Halves" (#185, 1/1/70). In his analysis of *Laverne and Shirley*, Alexander Doty (1993) sees the pregnancy motif in the American sitcom as one of its most profound feminist markers and sees this as a link between *I Love Lucy* and *Bewitched*:

> Integrating Lucille Ball's pregnancy into *I Love Lucy*'s text established a precedent and a pattern for having women-centered sitcoms use expectant motherhood to reinforce and expand the women-bonding aspects of their narratives. Far from shifting the series' emphasis toward heterosexual domestic concerns, as might be expected, the pregnancy and postpartum episodes of . . . *Bewitched* are concerned with marginalizing and trivializing male characters while (re)establishing a network of supportive women around the mother-to-be. (47)

Bewitched borrowed a number of story ideas from famous *I Love Lucy* episodes besides the pregnancy plotline. For example, the "Super Arthur" episode (#190, 2/5/70) features Uncle Arthur dressed up as Superman, which recalls the time Lucy dressed up as the man of steel for Little Ricky's birthday party ("Lucy and Superman," #166, 1/14/57). Sam and Darrin also go on a multiepisode trip to Europe at the beginning of season 8 (episodes 229–35) with Larry and Louise, replicating a European storyline featured on *I Love Lucy* with foreign travelers Lucy, Ricky, Fred, and Ethel (episodes 141–53). Sam and Darrin visit Italy, France, and England, catching major sites along the way such as Loch Ness, the Leaning Tower of Pisa, the Eiffel Tower, and an English castle, just as the Ricardos and the Mertzes travel to England and Scotland, Paris, the Swiss Alps, Italy (to allow Lucy to famously stomp grapes with the locals), and Monte Carlo.

Another *I Love Lucy* episode, "The Diet" (#4, 10/29/51), concerns one of Lucy's lamebrain schemes to become famous by performing at Ricky's nightclub. As it turns out, a spot is open for a dancer there, but she will have to fit the dress that is available for the number. Determined to go on stage, Lucy diets furiously so she will be able to fit into the dress on the big night. In his study of this episode, "The Cabinet of Lucy Ricardo," Alexander Doty (1990) asserts that much of *I Love Lucy* worked to "infantilize" Lucy: "Many *I Love Lucy* episodes are almost brutally insistent on reinforcing this 'woman-as-child' cultural code, even beyond exploiting Lucy's trademark bawling cry" (9). "The Diet" is a crucial exception to this, where Lucy is able to perform with talent and verve:

> The coda of "The Diet" presents one of the most pointed (and poignant) instances of the struggle between narrative demands and performance spectacle in the series, with Ball and her star image caught in the middle. Lucy's enter-

taining turn as Sally Sweet would have secured her a regular job at Ricky's club if she hadn't dieted herself to malnutrition to fit into a size 12 costume. Ball's Tiger Lily/Goldwyn Girl had the requisite figure as well as the talent, but poor Lucy Ricardo doesn't. (13)

On *Bewitched*, no such disconnect between star and performer occurs. Samantha Stephens is every bit as mature and talented as Elizabeth Montgomery.

Intriguingly, in one of Doty's source texts, the canonical feminist study of *I Love Lucy*, "Situation Comedy, Feminism, and Freud," Patricia Mellencamp does not mention *Bewitched*. Instead, she discusses the development of narrative and performative tensions in the history of the sitcom from *The George Burns and Gracie Allen Show* (CBS, 1950–58) to *I Love Lucy* to *The Dick Van Dyke Show* (CBS, 1961–66), the straight-laced doppelgänger of the campy *Bewitched*: "In situation comedy, pacification of women occurred between 1950 and 1960 without a single critical mention that the genre's terrain had altered: the housewife, although still ruling the familial roost, changed from being a humorous rebel or well-dressed, wise-cracking, naïve dissenter who wanted or had a paid job—from being out of control via language (Gracie) or body (Lucy)—to being a contented, if not blissfully happy, understanding homebody (Laura Petrie)" (81). In addition to attending to the passive Laura on *The Dick Van Dyke Show*, a feminist analysis of the 1960s sitcom should also include attention to the liberation of Samantha Stephens.

Lucy's concern over weight is of course silly: the idea that film star Lucille Ball would need to lose weight to conform to some artificial ideal (in this case the show dress) is patently absurd. Nonetheless, it is a hegemonic commonplace that in a patriarchal culture it is the woman who will complain about her weight while the husband insists she is being ridiculous. In this way, the patriarchal pressure to be thin is displaced onto the supposed vagaries of women. This trope is seen over and over again on television. To wit, in an episode of *The Cosby Show* (NBC, 1984–92), the beautiful and slender Clair Huxtable diets so that she will be able to fit into a sequined dress and win the "smooth" contest between her and her husband, Cliff (#34, "Clair's Toe," 12/5/85). Again, Cliff encourages her to buy the dress in a bigger size, but Clair insists that she should reduce to get back to her former size, which in her mind is the size she "should" be.

Similarly, Elizabeth Montgomery always looked great no matter what Sears and Roebuck outfit she happened to be sporting on *Bewitched*. However, rather than having to worry about just a few pesky pounds, Samantha balloons to over 500 pounds in the episode "Samantha Is Earthbound" (#244, 1/15/72). Luckily, because the witchcraft has actually just increased her density, she does not actually *look* any different; she just has a tough time lifting herself off the couch. Equally luckily, the pounds just melt right off when magic in the form of family witch doctor Dr. Bombay's (Bernard Fox) cure solves her witchcraft-induced problem.

The episode suggests that an overweight Sam is a disaster for the domestic bliss of the show. The normally energetic housewife is reduced to a helpless blob, unable to fulfill her mortal obligations of tending to her family and fixing last-minute dinners for the clients that Larry invariably invites over in an effort to secure another advertising contract. Although Sam's excessive weight gain lampoons a common obsession, an overweight housewife nonetheless threatens both marital bliss and business success. Dr. Bombay's cure is a bulimic extreme, "lightening up" Sam to the point that she floats. Weighing next to nothing, however, does make her a perfect model (for shoes that make the wearer feel as if they are "walking on air"), anorectic stuff that becomes the grist for another of Darrin's hypercommercial advertising slogans.

One other *Bewitched* storyline (the tooth fairy plot)

deals obliquely with weight reduction. The client in those episodes is a manufacturer of a cumbersome sauna/weight-reducing steam suit called the "Reduce-a-Lator." At the end of the episode, Samantha has been wearing the Reduce-a-Lator to hide the fairy wings she is stuck with, but when the suit malfunctions and she begins to overheat, Darrin, Larry, and client Mr. Ferber are forced to strip the contraption off the sweltering Sam. She steps out of the suit as a beautiful fairy, complete with white gossamer minidress and sparkly wings. The episode indicts suspect advertising promises for weight-loss gadgets (it is not likely that many of us would step out of the Reduce-a-Lator looking as beautiful as Samantha Stephens). Lucy had no better luck: the sauna gag references the *I Love Lucy* dieting episode discussed above, in which Lucy goes to a spa to use a steam cabinet, and in true Lucy style, gets stuck in it as the steam pours in.

Bewitched, in direct continuity with *I Love Lucy,* lays the critical soil for more pointed subsequent sitcom engagements with women's weight, most famously Roseanne Barr's. Using Mikhail Bakhtin's concept of the carnivalesque celebration of grotesquery, Kathleen Rowe describes Barr's performance in this way: "Arnold compounds her fatness with a looseness of body language and speech. She sprawls, slouches, and flops on furniture; her speech—even apart from its content—is loose, its enunciation and grammar 'sloppy,' and its tone and volume 'excessive'" (62). While Samantha's aristocratic upbringing does not make her a class equivalent of Roseanne, *Bewitched*'s feminist excesses have far more in common with Barr than they do with the more demure Laura Petrie.

Perhaps the clearest quotation from *I Love Lucy* is found in "Samantha's Power Failure" (#165, 3/20/69). Much of this episode directly remakes "Job Switching," one of the most famous episodes of *I Love Lucy,* and perhaps one of the most famous episodes ever of an American sitcom (#39,

9/15/52). In the *Bewitched* story, Samantha and Tabitha are stripped of their powers by the Witches' Council, a body that is once again irate that Samantha has dared to marry the mortal Darrin. In a show of solidarity, Sam's cousin Serena and uncle Arthur voice their support, and promptly lose their powers as well. The two new mortals are forced to get jobs, and are able to find entry-level employment at an ice cream store. This sets up the same premise as that found in "Job Switching," where Lucy and Ethel try their hand at employment to show they are "as good as the men." The two women famously end up at a candy factory where things go horribly wrong when they try to wrap candies coming ever faster off a conveyer belt. In the *Bewitched* episode, Serena and Uncle Arthur find themselves in front of the same conveyer belt that befuddled Ethel and Lucy in the candy factory. As expected, witch and warlock make a mess out of making chocolate-covered bananas in no time at all: here the witches' out-group status—gay man and witch without her powers— mimics the gender issues (women with no job skills) in Lucy's struggle for a public presence in 1950s America.

Bewitched and *I Love Lucy* also share a common element in that both shows touch on having family members advertise products to which the family patriarch has some connection. This can be seen in the *Bewitched* episode "Mother-in-Law of the Year" (#214, 1/14/71), which can be compared to the *I Love Lucy* episode "Lucy Does a TV Commercial" (#30, 5/5/52). Here, Lucy begs Ricky to let her be the spokesperson for a new nutritional supplement, the liquid "Vitameatavegamin." The commercial script calls for Lucy to discuss the product, then actually consume a spoonful at the end to demonstrate its wonderful taste. Multiple takes featuring the alcoholic potion soon take their toll, and Ball's marvelous performance as the increasingly drunk spokeswoman is of course a comedy classic. The "Mother-in-Law of the Year" *Bewitched* episode similarly features a disastrous commercial shoot, but the problems are caused by witchcraft rather than alcohol. When Endora, who is supposed to be the spokesperson in a candy commercial, fails to show up for filming, Samantha (as Endora) fills in for her. Hilarity ensues when Endora then shows up as Samantha, and Darrin has to do some fast talking about special effects to save the day. As this comparison indicates, *Bewitched,* as *I Love Lucy* before it, illustrates that everyday television, as much as modernist literature, is capable of engaging in auto-critique, in this case via deconstructions of the television commercials that invariably interrupt the fictional narratives.[5]

A second *Bewitched* episode involving one of Darrin's relatives pitching products for his clients on television is "Ho Ho the Clown" (#92, 1/12/67). In this story, Samantha, Tabitha, and Endora attend a taping of "Ho Ho the Clown," a television show sponsored by one of Darrin's clients. Endora is incensed that Tabitha is not eligible for the toy chest prize because of Darrin's involvement with the show and magically makes sure that Tabitha wins the prize anyway. She furthermore bewitches the clown himself so that he insists on having Tabitha at the next taping of the show so he can dote on his "cute little doll" on the air. When the client finds out that Tabitha is Darrin's child, he is furious and threatens to pull the account. Sam quickly solves the crisis when she zaps up a doll that looks identical to Tabitha, and tells the client that Ho Ho's antics were all a gag to produce interest in a new doll for the toy company.

Tabitha makes it onto television again in the episode "TV or Not TV" (#236, 11/3/71). In this episode, Tabitha and Adam are watching a Punch and Judy puppet show on television when Adam hits Tabitha. Upset at this senseless violence, Tabitha zaps herself into the show as it is airing live, and lectures the puppets on the bad example they are setting for children. Of course the show is sponsored by one of Darrin's clients, and complications arise when the producers love Tabitha and want her to become a series regular. Larry wants Tabitha to go on and increase ratings to make the client happy, but Tabitha soon tires of working on the show and wants to quit. Samantha solves the problem by magically convincing the client that his daughter, an aspiring actress, would be perfect to do the show instead.

Both these shows involving Tabitha working for Darrin's advertising clients on the air are critical of television. Ho Ho the Clown is a jaded actor when not on the air, similar to *The Simpsons'* Krusty the Clown, while the Punch and Judy show is needlessly violent. Furthermore, in the Ho Ho episode, Darrin is horrified when Tabitha wins the studio audience prize. He screams that he is going to end up in jail as a result of an FCC investigation (a clear reference to the quiz-show scandals of the 1950s). In all these examples, television is shown as a corrupt and corrupting influence on society.

Previous Criticism
of *Bewitched*

The current state of *Bewitched* criticism consists mostly of reductive analyses that typically focus on one representative episode, usually the pilot. A useful example is media scholar Christina Lane's entry on the show in the *Encyclopedia of Television,* which emphasizes *Bewitched's* formulaic nature: "*Bewitched's* formula typically involves a disruption created by either Samantha's or Darrin's family, or Darrin's boss Larry" (180). While many of the *Bewitched* episodes do in fact deal with disruptions caused by family members, such an analysis misses what I find most useful about a show such as *Bewitched.* What makes television interesting is not the formula itself, but television's capacity to deviate, restructure, and explode that formula within the realm of one textual universe we call a series. The 254 episodes of *Bewitched* present a plethora of such diverse situations, despite the popular perception of it as a "formula" show.

While academic television criticism has tended to be reductive, television fans, by contrast, obsess over the nuances of individual episodes and how they relate to the series as a whole. Pick up any fan book about a television show, or log onto any fan Web site, and one finds extensive discussions of individual episodes or aspects of a show (to wit, sound specialist Bill Lane's Web page on the evolution of the harp sound effect in *Bewitched*'s last five seasons). Now certainly, such discussion is often itself reductive, revolving around whether an episode passes muster with the fans or disappoints them. Regardless, the intensive *method* is still worth considering: fusing the formidable critical tools of academic criticism with the labor-of-love analyses by the viewing public can bring to light a rich tapestry of culture woven by the episodes of *Bewitched*.

Christina Lane is, of course, writing a short encyclopedia entry, and is careful to use the caveat of "typical" in presenting a formula for the *Bewitched* episodes. But her entry also offers another strategy that characterizes television studies' often reductive argumentation. Lane discusses the pilot as her textual example of the show as a whole: "The series premier remains one of the series' most memorable episodes in many ways" (181). Film analysis techniques are overlaid onto the discussion of the television text and, unwittingly, the television show is reduced to its most cinematic equivalent, the pilot (the "pilot film," it is often called). Such an analysis is necessarily incomplete, as it leaves undiscovered the eight years of character and cultural exploration that follow that initial show.

An examination of other *Bewitched* criticism reveals that most essays also follow a model inherited from the analysis of film and literature. David Marc, one of the most prolific and accomplished academic television critics, devotes only a few pages to his analysis of *Bewitched* in his book *Comic Visions: Television Comedy and American Culture.* Again reducing the show to one episode (#2, "Be It Ever So Mortgaged," 9/24/64), Marc notes, "In [the episode] much of the series' cosmos is delineated" (136). Marc presents *Bewitched* as a critically manageable unit with a stable political cant—it is a conservative show in its gender representations—and moves on to analyze other television shows. Indeed, not a single academic article or book has been published that is solely devoted to the analysis of *Bewitched.* The academic work on this show has all been part of essays devoted to large-scale analyses of the sitcom as a form. Ultimately, it is this very rhetorical form of sitcom criticism—an essay grappling with many texts rather than just one—that has perpetuated the reductionism of individual sitcoms.

Whereas essay- and even book-length analyses of individual films are standard in film studies, not many such works exist for individual television shows, particularly of 1960s telefilm sitcoms. Television studies still awaits its *Citizen Kane Book.* Here, ironically, film as a model is *not* embraced in television criticism. One finds the founding assumption of film studies (the television text is similar to the film text, as the film text is in turn the equivalent to the literary text), without the pivotal critical apparatus that supports that discipline. If one takes a cue from the success of film studies, then one must realize that in order to more fully understand these television texts, individual essay- and book-length studies will be needed to illuminate them.

The thrust of academic criticism for *Bewitched* and other television shows has been to grapple with one theme of a show at a time, often as part of a larger project. Lynn Spigel's essay, "From Domestic Space to Outer Space," uses *Bewitched* as part of a greater analysis of the space race and its figuration in 1960s sitcoms. But in doing so, she necessarily reduces most of the eight years of the show to a single line: "*Bewitched* employs the narrative conventions of the middle-class suburban sit-com. . . . Typically, Darrin Stephens has an important advertising account at the office, but his domestic situation leads to complications" (216).

To begin moving television studies toward a more synthetic rather than reductive criticism will require the abandonment of the quest for typicality. In fact, recent television demonstrates quite clearly that it is the medium's reliance on *atypical* episodes—defined as "very special episodes" during sweeps weeks—that drives its economic model. Atypical episodes ripe for academic interest abound: the live episode of *ER* (NBC, 1994–present), the musical episode of *Xena: Warrior Princess* (first-run syndication, 1995–2001), the final episode of *Newhart* (CBS, 1982–90), the World Trade Center episode of *The Simpsons,* and such. Anna McCarthy expertly studies the fabricated "media events" that have emerged in the U.S. television industry, particularly after the 1990s dominance of NBC's Thursday evening block, advertised as "Must See TV." McCarthy takes as her example the coming-out episode of the ABC sitcom, *Ellen* (#84, "The Puppy Episode," 4/30/97), a media event that fundamentally transformed the nature of the show and ultimately resulted in its cancellation the next season. McCarthy's analysis importantly pays attention to television's segmentation as a neglected part of what Raymond Williams refers to as the more dominant flow (140). McCarthy claims: "It is through the rupture of its own routine that television appears to have access to the momentary, the discontinuous, the real" (91). In this book, I will attend to individual *Bewitched* episodes, many of which—although certainly not all, perhaps not even most—partook of this access to the real: the moon landing, the civil rights movement, and the women's movement, to name a few.

37

Television critic Barry Putterman has considered the impoverished position into which the example of film has placed television criticism. Putterman correctly remarks, "Television criticism has always been the bastion of arrogantly sloppy generalists" (95). This admittedly angry assessment nonetheless applies to the *Bewitched* criticism. Even the critics who appreciate the show support their analyses with no more than a few episodes, perhaps unwittingly accepting the standard bias against the very 1960s telefilm sitcoms that they are working to reevaluate: that is, once you have seen a few episodes of a 1960s telefilm sitcom, you have seen them all.

Historically, there are reasons for this lack of attention to the complete runs of television series. More so than film, television has been considered a disposable artifact. The Museum of Broadcasting is lucky if it has a few episodes of any given TV show, while carefully restored VHS and DVD copies of a large number of major directors' entire oeuvres are readily available for home viewing. Although this is beginning to change with the release of boxed sets of entire seasons of a number of popular television shows, like *M*A*S*H* (CBS, 1972–83) and *Green Acres* (CBS, 1965–71), the difficulty in doing television criticism has always been the unavailability for study of the actual texts themselves. Many shows, particularly from the 1950s, are simply lost, never to be seen again.

In the specific case of *Bewitched,* lack of availability is not the problem. Clearly, *Bewitched* continues to fascinate, attracting new generations of fans who somehow connect with a show that is forty years old. As I researched this book starting in the early 1990s, *Bewitched* was airing between two and nine times per day (on cable outlets TBS and WGN, and on local stations), although some episodes air so rarely that it required a decade of searching to produce a full collection. The DVD boxed-set release is into its third season as of this writing. Indeed, *Bewitched* is one of the most successfully syndicated shows in television history, showing not only in the United States but also internationally. When I drafted the manuscript for this book in Berlin, the show was airing every weekend on Kabel 1, a particularly Americanized German cable television channel, as *Verliebt in eine Hexe* [*In Love with a Witch*]. The dubbing of the show's third season was done in 1966, and these episodes have been playing, intermittently, on German television ever since.

The contemporary reviews of *Bewitched* predict the academic response quite well. *TV Guide*'s Cleveland Amory responded to the pilot favorably: "The dinner party at Dick's old girl friend's was, in every sense of the word, pure magic— the season's high, in our opinion, in comedy shows so far" (A-54). Notably, Amory goes on to worry about the show quickly falling into formula, relying too much on witchcraft as a gimmick: "A little flies a long way and we like it used sparingly—for a special witching hour. Too much could start a witch hunt, and, who knows, we certainly wouldn't want the season's most diverting new show to end up having to call in a witch doctor" (A-54). By two seasons later, Ronald Searle was definitely not bewitched: "I know that the canned laughter underscoring these mournful lives in *Bewitched* is the laughter of lost souls. Who else would applaud so hysterically the words, 'What's for breakfast, Sam?' They know what's for breakfast. We are: sunny-side up" (18). In the popular criticism of the day, as in much of the academic criticism that was to follow, *Bewitched* was predictable formula, through and through.

A Sample Run
of *Bewitched* Episodes

While I discuss many episodes thematically throughout the rest of this book, I want to begin my analysis with a different method for establishing the variances of series television. Here I examine a string of episodes from the middle of the first season, whose nuanced shifting of the show's basic structure demonstrates the elegant possibilities of television textuality. While these episodes certainly represent a continuation of the narrative begun in the pilot, they also each engage a different set of questions posed by the show's initial premise, often contradicting other episodes in terms of the key features of the narrative universe.

Episode #22 of the first season, "Eye of the Beholder," in which Darrin purchases the antique "Maid of Salem" painting bewitched by Endora to show Samantha, provides a fruitful starting point. When Darrin realizes that Sam was just as youthful during the Salem witch trials in 1692, he questions the future of his marriage as he realizes that witches live for hundreds of years. The episode concludes with Samantha agreeing to not use her witch heritage to remain youthful, instead preferring to age "naturally" with Darrin. In one sense, this episode links back to the pilot, which asked the basic question of whether a marriage between a witch and a mortal could work at all. Samantha reveals herself to Darrin as a witch during the couple's honeymoon. "Eye of the Beholder" then continues this theme, asking the question of how such a relationship can endure as the (age) difference between them grows. Via this concern for things yet to come, "Eye of the Beholder" links to a set of episodes in *Bewitched* that project the show's characters into the future. The most recognizable of this grouping of episodes is "Samantha's Old Man" (#210, 12/3/70), in which Endora punishes Darrin by magically aging him until he is seventy-three years old. Samantha reassures Darrin by changing herself into a seventy-three-year-old woman, a scene for which the show received an Emmy award nomination for best makeup (Pilato 206). Here again, the show, now six seasons later, returns to the basic question of how this mixed marriage can possibly work.

The invocation of Salem links "Eye of the Beholder" to another grouping of *Bewitched* shows that grapple with the past. *Bewitched* is a show obsessed with history, featuring historical figures (Napoleon, Julius Caesar, Ben Franklin, and the like) zapped into the present, and main characters winking back into the past. In "Samantha Goes South for a Spell" (#142, 10/3/68), a vengeful witch sends Samantha as an amnesiac into antebellum New Orleans as punishment for her adultery with her husband (in fact, Sam's cousin Serena was the culprit). There, Samantha is befriended by a sassy African American maid, Aunt Jenny (played by Isabel Sanford, soon to be Louise of *The Jeffersons* [CBS, 1975–85]), who helps her defend her honor against the rapacious Rhett Butler clone, Rance, until Serena can zap Darrin back to rescue his wife (by kissing her—*Bewitched*'s unique cure for amnesia).

The specific invocation of the Salem witch trials in numerous episodes links *Bewitched*'s interest in history to its gender project. In terms of *Bewitched*'s stance on feminism, the critics of the show are evenly divided, with some emphasizing the conservative resolution of each individual episode (Samantha promises Darrin to obey him and never use magic again), while others note that, to maintain the long-term narrative, the next week this promise must be broken, thus empowering Samantha to override her husband's patriarchal prohibition against magic. The show's repeated invocation of the Salem witch trials as the cultural historical referent for Darrin's containment of Samantha's feminine power gives considerable weight to the latter critical position.

Back in the first season, the next episode, "Red Light, Green Light" (#23, 3/4/65), shifts the focus of the series to what I will call "Samantha's good citizenship." Samantha lobbies for a new traffic light to abate speeding on their suburban street, helped by Darrin who designs ads for their political rally. When the town's mayor refuses to approve the installation of the light, Samantha magically causes him to get stuck in a traffic jam, thus convincing him of the project's necessity. Unlike the pilot episode, here we have an episode in which Samantha's powers are used for social improvement; her marriage to Darrin takes a back seat to the use-value of magic to improve, not threaten, the mortal world.

The next week, the marriage returns to its central place in the narrative. In episode #24, "Which Witch Is Which" (3/11/65), Endora turns herself into Samantha so that she can stand in for her daughter at a dress fitting. A friend of Darrin's falls in love with Endora/Samantha, while snoopy neighbor Gladys Kravitz believes Samantha is cheating on Darrin. In the end, Endora saves the Stephens couple from embarrassment by convincing everyone concerned that she is indeed Samantha's twin.

In this episode, the trope of Samantha's meddling relatives who make trouble for Darrin, a stronger feature in later seasons, is added to the surveillance threat of Gladys Kravitz, the dominant concern of the first season. The real threat here, however, is to the Stephenses' marriage, with the devastating possibility of adultery in even the strongest of marriages driving the narrative. The episode also introduces the motif of doubling Samantha, which will most commonly be explored in the later episodes featuring cousin Serena. These episodes are important to a gender studies approach to *Bewitched*, as Serena represents feminism unfettered by the patriarchal imperatives of 1960s traditional femininity, and thus the show's repressed doppelgänger. That Sam's doppelgänger in "Which Witch Is Witch" is her mother, also harkens back to "Eye of the Beholder" (where Endora ages Darrin into an old man); in both, characters essentially switch generations as Darrin becomes old like Endora in "Eye of the Beholder" and Endora becomes young like Samantha in "Which Witch Is Which." In the latter particularly, witchcraft exacerbates oedipal tensions, enabling a man of Darrin's generation to fall in love with his mother-in-law.

The adultery threat continues in the next week's episode, "Pleasure O'Riley" (#25, 3/18/65), in which a beautiful model moves next door to the Stephenses' house on Morning Glory Circle. The model's boyfriend, a football player, mistakenly believes Darrin is romantically involved with Pleasure, forcing Samantha to use magic to protect her husband from harm. As in the previous episode, the threat of adultery lurks in the background of the Stephenses' marriage, but here the potential cuckold is Samantha, not Darrin. In this way, the show elegantly modulates its otherwise pedestrian adultery threat (to us, anyway, if not to 1960s viewers), shifting from Samantha to Darrin as the subject of taboo sexual desire.

In a show noted for the sweetness of its married couple protagonists, the next episode, "Driving Is the Only Way to Fly" (#26), discussed in the introduction, is notable for the vicious gender stereotyping, as Darrin oddly turns into a patriarchal bully while teaching Samantha to drive. While Endora again shows up in the episode as an invisible "back seat driver" to pressure Samantha into returning to her witch life, the biggest threat to the marriage in this instance appears to be Darrin himself.

The next episode changes gears again (so to speak), returning to the threat posed by Samantha's relatives in exposing her secret. In "There's No Witch like an Old Witch" (#27, 4/1/65), kindly Aunt Clara offers to babysit for Darrin's client's children, an ill-conceived idea that nearly exposes Samantha's identity; the elderly Aunt Clara's magic is only intermittently effective, and often uncontrollable.

In the episode that follows, Samantha's driving almost results in exposure again, linking back to "Driving Is the Only Way to Fly" from two episodes earlier. Circumventing the need for suburban gadgets devoted to "easy living," Samantha, too tired and rushed to get out of the car, uses her magic to zap the garage door open as she pulls into the driveway in "Open the Door Witchcraft" (#28, 4/8/65). When Mrs. Kravitz sees this, Darrin is forced to pretend they have just had installed a very expensive new garage door opener, a rarity at the time. When radio transmissions from aircraft flying over the house cause the door to open and close at inopportune moments, Darrin's vehement accusations of witchcraft (despite Sam's protests to the contrary) anger and hurt Samantha. Here, as in two episodes before, the threat magic poses to the marriage is superseded by Darrin's harsh patriarchal behavior toward his wife, assuming that her otherness (as woman and witch) is the cause of all his life's troubles.

In the next episode, "Abner Kadabra" (#29, 4/15/65), Samantha uses her magic to punish Mrs. Kravitz for her annoying snooping, offering the show's critique of surveillance culture, a motif I will explore later as one of the dominant obsessions of *Bewitched*'s many discursive strings. After Gladys sees Samantha using magic to rearrange paintings on her wall, Samantha uses some simple witchcraft tricks and some clever talking to convince the snoop that she must have extra sensory perception. Soon, however, things get out of hand as Mrs. Kravitz starts to believe she has all sorts of powers. Finally, Sam has to put an end to it all by turning Abner Kravitz (George Tobias) into dust, which Gladys is horrified to think she accomplished by telling her husband to "dry up." The episode was later remade with Darrin's mother, Mrs. Stephens, in the role of the hapless victim of Samantha's "ESP explanation," in "Samantha and the Antique Doll" (#228, 4/22/71).

The Kravitzes are featured as the main narrative focus three episodes later, continuing the surveillance trope by threatening to expose Samantha's secret. In "Illegal Separation" (#32, 5/6/65), Abner finally has enough of Gladys's kooky antics and moves in with Sam and Darrin. Knowing this will prove disastrous to their attempts to maintain secrecy, Darrin asks Samantha to use her magic to solve the crisis. Samantha does so by making both Abner and Gladys dream of the early, courting days of their relationship.

In the intervening two episodes, the potential of adultery returns yet again to threaten the Stephenses' marriage. In "George the Warlock" (#30, 4/22/65), the Pleasure O'Riley household, first introduced five episodes earlier, again tempts Darrin. With Pleasure away on a vacation, her sister, similarly allegorically named Danger, throws herself at Darrin. Endora uses this distraction to allow a warlock to resume wooing Samantha. While Darrin does not succumb to Danger's temptation, and Samantha rejects George's advances, the next episode, "That Was My Wife" (#31, 4/29/65), continues the first season's obsession with adultery as the central threat to a young married couple's life.

Darrin and Samantha decide to spend a romantic night together at a hotel in New York City. Yet when Larry spots Darrin with a black-haired woman in the hotel lobby (it is Samantha trying out her sexy new wig), Larry believes Darrin is cheating on his wife. Samantha's secret is almost discovered when she magically teleports herself back to their house in Connecticut to retrieve a book she has left behind, only to answer the door to Larry, who has come to console her in her time of grief. Here, unlike the other adultery-themed episodes, the normal mortal threat to a marriage is grafted onto the show's basic premise that Samantha's witchcraft can get Darrin into trouble with his boss, because as a businessman, he can afford to cheat on his wife, but his career can never withstand being deemed abnormal by conformist American culture.

In the next episode, and the last one that I will discuss from the first season, "A Change of Face" (#33, 5/13/65),

Samantha uncharacteristically joins in with Endora's trouble-making. While Darrin sleeps, the mother and daughter team of mischievous witches magically transform Darrin's face, rendering him more aesthetically pleasing in their eyes. In a show that would suddenly replace the actor (Dick York), who played Darrin for five seasons, with a completely different actor, Dick Sargent, without any diegetic explanation, this early episode details the instability between people's appearances and their true characters. In the conclusion, I will discuss *Bewitched*'s peculiar narrative operating rules and the significance they have for the show's intertextual place in television history by focusing on the show's handling of the replacement of the actor playing its central male protagonist. For now, however, I have discussed this twelve-episode run in such detail to highlight the show's elegant nuancing of the basic premises announced in the pilot. While a preponderance of these episodes highlight the pilot's basic question—can a mortal man have a successful marriage with a witch wife?—via plotlines about adultery, other episodes develop the show's premise in different directions. "Red Light, Green Light" allows a focus on Samantha's abilities to forward social causes (a tendency that would become more political later in the show as Sam worked magic for race relations and UNICEF, for example).

"Driving Is the Only Way to Fly" and "Open the Door Witchcraft" break quite severely with the show's loving premise, revealing a quite inflexible and mean-spirited Darrin, once one of his male domains, in this case driving, is invoked. "Open the Door Witchcraft" also demonstrates the show's ridiculing of television's bread and butter, technological gadgets advertised during the commercials, since Samantha can do anything the gadgets can with the mere twitch of her nose. More than a few episodes highlight the central concern of season 1: as the threat that the surveillance state poses to individual, seemingly free, cold war citizens, so does

Gladys Kravitz represent the hysterical threat posed to the Stephenses' nonconformist lifestyle. These multiple and interweaving themes can only be appreciated by a more global analysis of the show, an analysis that would be missed if only one or a few episodes were considered.

One of the first academics ever to write analytically about television textuality provides a model for appreciating the nuances in plot construction and ideology that this analysis of the twelve episodes in season one of *Bewitched* invokes. In his essay on *Magnum, P.I.* (CBS, 1980–88), Horace Newcomb presents a vision of television textuality that I will build on to analyze the multiplicity of *Bewitched*'s textual systems. Arguing for the merits of the detective show *Magnum, P.I.* over and above *Hill St. Blues* (NBC, 1981–87) and other contemporary "quality television" offerings, Newcomb tries to explain why almost all other reviewers have preferred the other shows ("*Magnum*").

Here and elsewhere, by "quality television" I refer to the 1970s and 1980s shows that relied on film style aesthetics and interwoven narratives about workplace families. The clearest definition of this type of quality television can be found in Thomas Schatz's study of *St. Elsewhere* (NBC, 1982–88). By "everyday television," I mean to coin a term that describes everything else that features no pretensions toward this narrow definition of quality. Newcomb contends that the critical preference for quality television has to do with its settling into pessimistic and ironic perspectives toward its material: "[The] wonderful narrative experiments of [*Hill St. Blues* and *St. Elsewhere*] are now used primarily to rework again and again successful formulas—with the familiar world-wise, world-weary perspective, with irony as a way of being, with cynicism that passes for humor" (24). In contrast, Newcomb sees *Magnum, P.I.* as engaging in a wide array of different perspectives on its diverse material:

Extending beyond Magnum and his compatriots, the show has created a broad and varied fictional world. It is a world filled with the most conventional detective-story components—threatening thugs, lost children, and wandering spouses. It is a world crammed with humor, from slapstick to wordplay. And it is a world grounded in melodrama of the first order, inviting us to be as concerned about character, values, and emotions as about adventure and mystery. (23)

Newcomb uses this unconventional view of *Magnum, P.I.*'s heterogeneity versus quality television's monolithic nature to explain the critical bias against everyday television: "This range of styles, in fact, may account for some of the perplexity on the part of reviewers. Tuning in on any given night they might encounter one of several *Magnum, P.I.*s. Unless they return for some of the others they may miss the program's true innovations" (23–24). For Newcomb, *Magnum* offers a portrayal of humanity every bit as compelling, perhaps even more so, than any critically lauded "quality" show that has graced the airwaves.

Newcomb sees *Magnum, P.I.* as an example of what he calls "cumulative narrative . . . a new television form that stands between the traditional self-contained episodic forms and the open-ended serials. . . . One episode's events can greatly affect later events, but they're seldom directly tied together. Each week's program is distinct, yet each is grafted onto the body of the series, its characters' pasts" (24). Newcomb sees the cumulative narrative as an innovation in television in the mid-1980s (his other example is *Cagney and Lacey* [CBS, 1982–88]), in contrast to the "traditional series," of which the 1960s telefilm sitcom would stand as one of the archetypes.

Although Newcomb suggests that *Magnum P.I.* is a special show that only became possible in the 1980s, I instead believe the same strengths of *Magnum* can be found much earlier in series television, and that these features are certainly not limited to this one popular detective show. I suggest that the commonality between *Magnum P.I.* and *Bewitched* lies in their status as everyday television. While quality television attempts to separate itself from the rest of the television landscape by rendering weekly "event" narratives, everyday television works within the week-to-week flow of the medium and works from within that flow to produce satisfying, yet unremarkable (by the standards of quality television) narratives. Magnum's struggle with the memory of his father and of Vietnam while stranded out at sea in "Home from the Sea" (#64, 9/29/83) is clearly about the issues of history and memory that Newcomb analyzes in his essay. Yet these issues are presented obliquely, to enrich the main plot, which is about Magnum staying afloat in the ocean in a desperate struggle for survival after he is separated from his sailboard. I suggest that as with *Magnum*, *Bewitched* uses everyday television strategies to deal with the important contemporary issues of the day.

A comparison between *ER* and *Bewitched* illuminates the difference between the way quality and everyday television shows present contemporary social issues such as racial politics. Two episodes of *ER*, a quality television show elevated into event status by NBC's "Must See TV" advertising strategy, are illuminating here. One features a direct depiction of racial discrimination against African Americans. In this episode (#17, "The Birthday Party," 2/16/95) the African American Dr. Peter Benton (Eriq LaSalle) is required by his job to treat a wounded racist (known as such because he has the words "Die Nigger Die" tattooed on his arm). Another intriguing episode (#64, "Tribes," 4/10/97) has white Dr. Greene (Anthony Edwards) preferentially treating a white victim over a black one because he assumes the latter is a gang member who shot the former. When it instead turns out

Sam as a civil rights protester, in "The Witches Are Out" (10/29/64).

that it was a black high school basketball star who was attacked by a white drug dealer, quality television forces both Dr. Greene and (the mostly white) audience members to examine their own racist assumptions.

Although quality television is praised for its depiction of important cultural issues such as race relations, everyday television also handles such topics, and *Bewitched* certainly tackled them also. The depiction, however, is much more covert. Instead of melodramatizing confrontation to achieve the "event" narrative, everyday television grapples with similar thematic issues in narrative structures that blend into television's flow. Samantha's confrontation with a Halloween goods manufacturer in "The Witches Are Out" (#7, 10/29/64) over stereotypical representations of witches is clearly about racial discrimination, but the theme is wrapped in an easy-to-swallow comedic piece about Halloween candy.

In grappling with weighty cultural matters (whether it be the trauma of Vietnam or discrimination in society), neither *Magnum, P.I.* nor *Bewitched* hyperdramatizes these situations. Whereas quality television such as *ER* and *Hill St. Blues* stand out from the shows around them via their aggressive aesthetic and narrative techniques, *Magnum, P.I.* and *Bewitched*, as everyday television, fit snugly into the overall flow of the schedule. They are not marketed for their realism, Emmy wins, or quality, but rather as entertaining shows.

Here, I have applied Newcomb's argument about the use-value of *Magnum* as a "quality show" (but distinctly not *quality television*) to *Bewitched*. Interestingly, though, Newcomb distinguishes *Magnum* as narratively more complex than other television shows, and it is here that I part company with his model of television textuality. While Newcomb argues for the narrative complexity of *Magnum, P.I.* over a simplistic 1960s telefilm narrative style, I believe the links between *Magnum, P.I.* and *Bewitched* as everyday television are stronger than their differences. What Newcomb argues about *Magnum, P.I.*'s attraction as cumulative narrative is true of all good television, everyday, quality, or otherwise.

The two features of the cumulative narrative that Newcomb finds so compelling in *Magnum, P.I.*—intimacy and the expansion into the past—are both present in *Bewitched*. First, Newcomb argues that intimacy with the characters distinguishes the cumulative narrative: "Satisfying familiarity and intimacy results from the powerful narrative economy available in a cumulative series" ("*Magnum*" 24). Second, a cumulative narrative includes the expansion into the past: "Cumulative series expand into the past, explaining how the characters got to this place. In one sense, these series are about their own pasts" (25). Both of these criteria apply as much to *Bewitched*, a "traditional" series, as they do to *Magnum, P.I.* Without the intimate relationship with the characters, I would not feel compelled to see every episode, nor

51

would I want to see anew episodes that I have already seen again and again. Furthermore, I believe the second criterion, the expansion into the past, is what makes *Bewitched* one of the most interesting and important shows in the history of television.

Valuing 1960s Telefilm Aesthetics

While much of the argumentation of this book concerns narrative and ideological matters, I now want to attend to the way in which *Bewitched* functions aesthetically. Evaluation of the aesthetics of the situation comedy ought to properly begin with David Barker's article, "Television Production Techniques as Communication." First published in 1985 in *Critical Studies in Mass Communication,* Barker uses his comparative study of the visual aesthetic practices of *M*A*S*H* (shot film style, with one camera, out of continuity and therefore without a live studio audience) and *All in the Family* (shot "proscenium style," with multiple cameras, in continuity with a live studio audience) to demonstrate his thesis: "the communicative ability of any television narrative is, in large part, a function of the production techniques utilized in its creation" (170).

Barker's choice to analyze two early 1970s "Television Renaissance" shows is crucial for understanding the history of television studies against which I have been intervening in order to frame a serious analysis of *Bewitched,* a sitcom shot neither proscenium style as *All in the Family* nor film style as *M*A*S*H,* but with what Barker refers to as "1960s telefilm values" (170). Traditional sitcom history, on which Barker relies, presents a story in which early proscenium experimentation (*I Love Lucy* and *The Honeymooners* [CBS, 1955–56]) gave way to cheap, assembly-line efficiency (1960s telefilm sitcoms like *Gilligan's Island* and *Bewitched*).

In 1963, President Kennedy's Federal Communications Commissioner Newton Minnow delivered his famous "Vast Wasteland" speech, in which he challenged television industry workers to sit down for a day and actually watch their programming. He insisted that they would not be able to stomach the rubbish that was being broadcast. It is typically proposed that the effects of the speech were limited to a short-lived increase in documentary production and public service programming, as a strategy by the networks to shield the moneymaking sitcoms from any direct reform.[6] Otherwise, fictional programming in the 1960s is seen to have continued under the status quo with airing of the "vast wasteland" sitcoms such as the barnyard oddities of producer Paul Henning. As Ella Taylor analyzes, "Once the anxiety generated by Minnow's speech had died down, competition between the networks to fill the prime-time schedules with new comic gimmicks escalated to fever pitch. Among the results were spooky families, adult cartoons . . . and people with magical powers" (29).

The "Television Renaissance" of the early 1970s, then, provided an artistic reaction against television's 1960s "vast wasteland." Despite the fact that the three sitcom triumphs of the renaissance period—*All in the Family, M*A*S*H,* and *The Mary Tyler Moore Show*—used remarkably different techniques to implement this rebellion, Barker uses similar terms to describe their victory over the cheapness of the 1960s techniques. Barker presents *M*A*S*H,* despite its having being shot with one camera, like *Bewitched,* as a subtle and precise use of the medium:

> Other times, however, the relationships were far more subtle, as when Charles, who has been talking to Hawkeye and B. J., turns his head toward the door of the Swamp and we cut to a moment later that day as Hawkeye and B. J. leave the Swamp and walk outside. In either case, how-

ever, it was the preciseness with which these words and actions were matched through editing (and judicious shot selection) that allowed the viewer to not only jump across space and time with no loss of orientation but to likewise make the comedic connection between a stranded Potter and Klinger and an amorous Hawkeye. (175)

When in turn discussing *All in the Family,* shot with multiple cameras before a live studio audience, Barker uses the same language of artistic valuation: "In a scene this involved, precise execution of blocking and dialogue—both matters of timing—was essential. Any lapse in this execution would have prevented the director from getting the necessary shot" (176). Against these attributions of precision and subtlety, the 1960s telefilm values are deemed "highly utilitarian" and "repetitive and predictable" (170).

Barker's analyses of *M*A*S*H* and *All in the Family* are indeed compelling. However, a show like *Bewitched,* shot on a soundstage with one camera, out of continuity in order to minimize production costs, is not so very different from a show like *M*A*S*H.* Unquestionably, the depth of *M*A*S*H*'s sets did enable the elegant crossing of multiple plot lines, as Barker maintains, but it is equally true that *Bewitched* employed its one-camera shooting style to interesting effects, effects impossible within the multiple-camera proscenium shooting technique that is valorized in Barker's analysis of *All in the Family.*

I want to explore this assertion by engaging a relatively detailed comparison of the *Bewitched* episode discussed earlier, "Samantha's Power Failure," and its counterpart in sitcom history, the "Job Switching" episode of *I Love Lucy.* In each case, the main characters decide to go outside of the home in order to get jobs in the public sphere. And, in each case, the aesthetic practices produce comic effects through the televisual development of narrative. *I Love Lucy,* along with *The Honeymooners,* pioneered the multiple-camera shooting technique on a soundstage that presented itself to a live audience as if it were a play, hence the appellation of "proscenium" style shooting. This innovation allowed for sparkling comedic timing, as theatrically trained actors could play off of one another while delivering performances housed in continuity with the story being developed. Such is the case with the first act of "Job Switching," the premiere episode of *I Love Lucy's* second season.

The episode begins with Ricky (Desi Arnaz) storming into the Ricardo apartment, walking into a frontal medium shot with his arms crossed. He is upset because Lucy has once again overdrawn their bank account. A cut follows a happy Lucy (Lucille Ball) walking onto the set, about to give her husband a kiss. When she notices Ricky is upset with her, she turns away from him. Another cut, this time to the left-most camera—*I Love Lucy's* multiple camera technique employed three cameras, which I will designate left, center, and right—offers an elegant composition in depth, with worried Lucy in the foreground and angry Ricky in the background.

Ricky explains that he has just returned from the bank. This sets up the first joke of the episode. Ricky reads the back of Lucy's check written to the beauty parlor: "Dear teller, be a lamb, and don't put this through until next month." The visual coverage of this line is delivered by the left camera, a simulation of an over-the-shoulder two-shot, frontal on Ricky, three-quarters on Lucy's face. As Lucy delivers her comic riposte—"That's why they call them tellers, they go around blabbing everything they know"—the editor cuts to the right camera, in the proscenium equivalent to a reverse angle, wherein now all of Lucy's face is presented, with Ricky one-half obscured. The sequence continues, cut together between these two camera positions, visually demonstrating the financial argument between Lucy and Ricky.

Then, the Ricardos' friends and neighbors, the Mertzes, arrive. Ricky has backed Lucy into the front corner of the set, covered by the left camera. We see the Mertzes enter through the front door, in the background of the shot. The editor cuts to the center camera to deliver a medium shot of Fred and Ethel, who try to leave—Fred jokes, "No thanks, I went to the fights last night"—once they realize they have stumbled upon a domestic squabble. The editor cuts back to the left camera as Ricky and Lucy coax their friends into the living room for mediation. As all four performers find their marks, the left camera finds them in *plan americain* (from the knees up), with Ricky closest to the camera screen left, forming a line with Fred, Ethel, and Lucy farther to screen right.

The visual rhetoric of the scene immediately changes, as there is a cut to the right camera, revealing Ricky putting his arm around Fred in a medium shot. Ricky asks, "How often is Ethel's checking account overdrawn?" When Fred replies, "Never," the editor cuts to the left camera, framing a medium shot of Ethel and Lucy, the latter of whom grimaces in what she assumes to be the devastation of her rhetorical position. Lucy is redeemed with Ethel's quip: "I never had enough money at one time to open a checking account." At this point, the editor cuts to the center camera, which re-frames the four-shot *plan americain:* in the background of this image, we see Lucy's broad smile at the comic redemption of her position.

Even before the dialogue of the show has stated its premise—another battle of the sexes plotline, in this case Ricky and Fred will stay home to take care of the housework while Ethel and Lucy will go find jobs in the public sphere—the visual aesthetics have divided the characters into two-shots framing the men against the women. The center camera captures the four-shot as Fred initiates the show's first turning point, the idea of job switching. Fred observes: "Let's face it, Rick. When it comes to money, there are two kinds of people, the earners and the spenders. Or as they are more popularly known, husbands and wives." As Fred finishes his line, the editor cuts to the left camera to capture Lucy scoffing and tapping Ethel on the shoulder. The editor cuts back to the right camera as Ricky states that women would spend less if they had to earn the money. The first act ends with an elegant ballet of cutting between these three shots (Ricky and Fred voicing patriarchy, Lucy and Ethel rebelling against it, and all four of them together).

This first act of "Job Switching" is one of the clearest examples of the artistic value of multiple camera proscenium shooting. However, *Bewitched*'s telefilm style is equally artistic. The best example of this is in *Bewitched*'s one-camera reconstruction of the first act of "Job Switching" in "Samantha's Power Failure." The episode begins with a teaser in which Endora informs Samantha that the witches' council has revoked her powers due to her marriage to the mortal Darrin. Sam tries to move flowers on the breakfast table using magic, but a funny sound effect indicates that her magic is on the fritz. Endora pops in and diagnoses Sam as suffering from a "power failure."

Next, Uncle Arthur pops up (literally, out of the toaster). As Sam walks over to him, the camera delivers an over-the-shoulder two-shot, manipulated with special effects such that Sam is full size but Arthur 3 inches tall, a direct effect of film-style shooting, as such manipulation would be impossible with live, in-continuity proscenium techniques. Sam's cousin Serena pops into the living room, to practice her karate on Sam's coffee table. Since Elizabeth Montgomery also plays Serena, one-camera, out-of-continuity film shooting also allows Serena and Samantha to appear in the same scene, an impossibility with proscenium shooting.

Now "Samantha's Power Failure" begins to deliver a one-camera version of the first act of "Job Switching." This sequence begins with a medium shot of Serena, who has broken Sam's table in the living room with a powerful karate chop. Sam, Arthur, and Endora walk into the room to investigate the loud noise. Serena snaps her fingers and the table magically repairs itself. Because this image is produced by reversing the film, this technique would also have been impossible with proscenium shooting.

Endora walks over to Serena, and the blocking reiterates that in *I Love Lucy* as the characters separate into pairs. Endora and Serena are seen in one two-shot, while Arthur and Sam are left behind standing in the dining room in the other shot. Endora tries to get Arthur and Serena to leave: "Samantha and I are trying to have a serious discussion." But Arthur refuses: "We know all about that, Endora. That's why we're here."

The character relationships visually realign as Serena walks over to Arthur and the camera now features them in a two-shot together. This action leaves Sam alone in the dining room. The editor cuts back to the two-shot of Arthur and Serena. Serena reassures Sam that, "We're behind you 100 percent." Arthur chimes in: "And don't let those old crones at the council split you and Darrin."

Now it is Endora who is alone, sitting in a chair. She uses vindictive magic to literally button Arthur's lips and zip Serena's mouth shut. Samantha then convinces Endora to undo this spell, and Endora complies. This sequence, again, would not work if shot proscenium style, because the special effects require the camera to stop while actors or props are moved in front of or away from the camera (in this case, the zipper and button on the lips of Serena and Arthur). After a loud thunderclap, Endora gloats because she now knows that Arthur's and Serena's powers have been taken away as well. Arthur tries to perform his famous tablecloth trick, but without his magic, he destroys all of Sam's dishes. Similarly, Serena hurts her hand karate chopping the table. After this action, the camera reveals Serena and Arthur together again in their two-shot. As Endora pops out triumphantly, Arthur continues to reassure Sam: "Don't worry Sammy, everything is going to be fine. We'll get jobs and function just like mortals."

Arthur and Serena walk over to Sam, forming a brief three-shot together, indicating that they are all unified in having lost their powers. However, as the first act ends, the shots alternate between a medium close-up of Sam alone and the two-shot of Arthur and Serena, a visual indication that Sam knows as well as we do that while she can live in the mortal world, the most likely outcome for Arthur and Serena is disaster.

"Samantha's Power Failure" delivers an almost identical plot development as found in "Job Switching" while using antithetical aesthetic techniques. In each case, an elegant set of shots is employed to visually indicate the character alignments produced by these new plot circumstances. If anything, the *Bewitched* episode is more interesting since it develops a surprisingly new alignment between Arthur and Serena *against* Endora. In a reductive description of *Bewitched*, Endora, Arthur, and Serena would be lumped together as interchangeable antagonists who, as witches, threaten the mortal Darrin. However, this episode breaks with that formula. Here, Arthur and Serena line up on Sam's side, against the meddling of Endora and the witches' council. Conversely, in many episodes of *I Love Lucy*, not just "Job Switching," Ethel joins Lucy in her hair-brained schemes to break into the public sphere against Ricky's wishes.

I choose this one comparison with which to begin an analysis of the aesthetic practices of the telefilmed *Bewitched* because the plot circumstances of the "job switching" episodes offer such a direct contrast between *Bewitched*'s 1960s telefilm one-camera technique with *I Love Lucy*'s vaunted proscenium shooting technique. Many episodes of *Bewitched* demonstrate an artistic deployment of aesthetic practices that are as valuable as those in *M*A*S*H*, a show whose one-camera aesthetic practice has been praised. Interestingly, though, the contributions of *Bewitched*'s aesthetic practices have been dismissed. Barker implies that *M*A*S*H* artistically utilized the power of film-style shooting while 1960s telefilm sitcom shooting (a generalization that would include *Bewitched*) merely used the efficiency of one-camera techniques to minimize production costs.

Like *M*A*S*H*, *Bewitched*'s production techniques produced many narrative and ideologically meaningful visual images. For example, in "Be It Ever So Mortgaged," the second episode of the series, Sam and Endora go to visit 1164 Morning Glory Circle, the address at which Sam and Darrin would live for the entire series. The scene is shot on location, before a real house on a real street. The editor cuts from an exterior shot of the house to a two-shot of Sam and Endora. Sam loves the house; Endora finds it "filthy." The editor then cuts to snoopy neighbor Gladys excitedly looking out her window, checking out the new arrivals. Here we see the first instance of Gladys seeing magic not meant for mortals to see. Soon she is hysterical after watching Sam and Endora magically zap in different landscapes, and convinces Abner to come look at the yard instantly materialized around the Stephenses' home. Of course, by the time Abner looks, all of the evidence of Sam's and Endora's magical interventions have been erased: they have moved on to look inside the house, and Abner forces Gladys to take her psychiatric medicine.

The show delivers no over-the-shoulder shot with Gladys in the foreground and Sam and Endora in the background—in other words, Gladys and husband Abner are shot in a separate space, the studio. It does rely on the flexibility of film production techniques, though, to cut back and forth between Sam the watched and Gladys the watcher. With the exception of jokes on the history of proscenium shooting—

such as the hidden face of Wilson, Tim Allen's neighbor on *Home Improvement*—proscenium shows rely on neighbors coming into the set of the main character (typically someone's home, be it the Conners' on *Roseanne* or the Cosbys'). *Bewitched,* conversely, relies on film shooting to differentiate Sam's magical world from Gladys's suburban one, the collapse of which would cause the ruination of Sam, our amiable protagonist.

Perhaps no episode better demonstrates the power of telefilm visual aesthetic practices over standard proscenium shooting than "A Vision of Sugar Plums" (#15, 12/24/64). In this, the show's first Christmas episode, both Gladys and Samantha have agreed to adopt an orphan for the holiday weekend. Late in the episode, Gladys's charge, Michael, brings over his fire engine for Tommy, Samantha's guest, to play with. In a high angle long shot, Gladys snoops on them from her upstairs window. Given standard sitcom aesthetics, the vertical dimension of the snooping is quite remarkable. In all of the proscenium shows in the history of television, the set is built on a first-story plane. While there is an upstairs in, say, Archie Bunker's house, and some bedroom scenes do in fact take place there, these scenes are performed on single-story special sets that are brought out for this purpose. The power of *Bewitched*'s telefilm shooting style is that it can explore the vertical dimension of suburban life, in this case, the power of Gladys to spy on Samantha in all three dimensions.

As for set design, the threat of Gladys's surveillance helps explain why, of all the sitcoms in the history of television, the Stephenses' foyer is so crucial to the show. Indeed, other sitcoms have included front doorways. Most proscenium domestic family sitcoms have shallow, wide sets (what Barker calls x-axis dominant sets) that feature a doorway on the right, a living room, and then a kitchen on the left. *All in the Family* is an important case, since that front door on the

Gladys Kravitz (Alice Pearce) snoops on the children, in "A Vision of Sugar Plums" (12/24/64).

right-hand side of the set also connected Archie's private bigotry to the changing world around him, which, crucially, the show did not represent directly. Instead, Archie's villains, like the liberal politician Claire Packard, would invade Archie's home and argue with him in his living room.

Bewitched spent an inordinate amount of time at the Stephenses' front door. This is because the doorway represents, through set design, the barrier between the external, mortal world and the private life in which Darrin fends off Samantha's and her relatives' witchcraft. The front door and its foyer served as Darrin's last line of defense against the revelation of Sam's secret to, at first, Gladys Kravitz and later, his boss, Larry Tate. As a set design issue, the foyer was the most remarkable change in the Stephenses' household, backed at first by a Rembrandt painting knock-off and then by a mirror, in which, in one episode, Maurice trapped Darrin.

As my primary example of the importance of the foyer,

I want to assess in detail one of the show's most notable episodes, "Sisters at Heart" (#213, 12/24/1970), a Christmas show written by a high school English class, in which Tabitha fights racial discrimination by zapping black-and-white polka dots onto her own skin as well as that of her African American friend. The episode is a remarkable example of *Bewitched*'s liberal politics. Aesthetically, its film style shooting accomplishes its goals with visual precision, with three crucial scenes in the episode that occur at the Stephenses' foyer.

Larry has brought Keith, his African American employee, over to Darrin's house, along with Keith's wife, Dorothy, and daughter, Lisa. Lisa introduces herself to Darrin, and is precociously polite, as if out of a scene from *Guess Who's Coming to Dinner* (1967). Tabitha is happy that she and Lisa are going to be "temporary sisters" while Keith leaves town for a few days to work on another account for Larry. Meanwhile, Darrin is trying to land the Brockway account, causing Larry to quip that if they can land both accounts, "We'll really have a white Christmas." The actor playing Keith is forced to deliver a lame racial joke: "Watch that!" In the second foyer scene, Darrin's client, Mr. Brockway, visits the Stephenses' household because his mother told him always to "check out a man's home life, make sure there aren't any skeletons rattling around in the closet." As Sam is upstairs tending to Adam, Lisa answers the door to Mr. Brockway. In a remarkable example of *Bewitched* director William Asher's skillful understanding of film aesthetics, the camera is placed right in the doorway, on-axis between Lisa and Brockway. Upon seeing Lisa, the racist Brockway attempts to explain away his surprise: "I'll bet your mommy is the housekeeper." Lisa asserts proudly that her father works for McMann and Tate, and that Tabitha is her sister. When Lisa invites Brockway in, he leaves, mumbling: "I think I've seen enough."

Lisa closes the door, ending the awkward scene in a close-up of a bright red Christmas ribbon on the door, to emphasize that Brockway's racism is in direct contrast to the spirit of the season. Aesthetically, the scene is shot as a high stakes moment, with the camera caught on the dramatic axis, placing us helplessly between the sweet little girl, Lisa, and the racist Brockway, with no one around to intervene. The camera work here is one the great triumphs of 1960s telefilm aesthetics, regardless of the saccharine simplicity of the show's liberal racial politics. A proscenium show simply could not deliver this camera work: at best, the multiple cameras could simulate over-the-shoulder two-shots, but the audience would be safely kept from the tension between Lisa and Brockway since the cameras never enter the performer space. At this moment, as in *M*A*S*H*—for example, in an early episode in which Hawkeye berates a soldier for referring to Koreans as "gooks" while in the presence of Spearchucker, an African American doctor—the one-camera production technique places the spectator right in the midst of the tension-filled racial drama.

"Sisters at Heart" saves its best use of the foyer—*Bewitched*'s space of indeterminacy, a boundary between private magic and public norms—for last. In the show's epilogue, Mr. Brockway returns to the Stephenses' house to apologize. The final scene begins in a long shot of the back of the Stephenses' living room, decorated with a large Christmas tree. Keith's family and Darrin's are opening presents. The doorbell rings. Samantha walks to the door and opens it to find Mr. Brockway. In a reprise of the first act set-up (perhaps shot at the same time, if telefilm efficiency is indeed the motor force of the 1960s production aesthetic), the camera is placed in the doorjamb, between Brockway and Samantha. This time, however, Brockway holds his hat in his hand, repentant. Sam stands speechless as Brockway struggles to express himself.

Sam invites him in, taking him by the shoulder and drawing him into the living room while sending the children upstairs. In medium close-up, Brockway addresses all four adults, explaining that he could not sleep because of the strange experience he had at the Stephenses' the day before. In that earlier scene, Sam cast a spell on Brockway, causing him to see everyone, including Darrin and Larry (played by the white actors in blackface!), as African Americans. "Sisters at Heart" participates in the problematic history of blackface on American television, including the infamous blackface episode of *Gimme A Break!* (NBC, 1981–87).

Brockway is improbably transformed by this experience. He explains: "I discovered something about myself. I found out that I'm a racist." Things end happily as Keith accepts Brockway's apology with an odd aphorism: "A very smart man said, to adequately define a problem is the first step toward solving it." Sam invites Brockway to stay for Christmas dinner. Sam explains that it will be a test: "A lot depends upon how you do at dinner. We're having integrated turkey. White meat and dark," a line used years later by Spike Lee in the Thanksgiving scene in *She's Gotta Have It* (1986).

Whatever one thinks about *Bewitched*'s naïve and simplistic liberalism, the show ends with an aesthetic tour de force. As they all laugh over this "joke," Sam, Brockway, and Darrin stand before the Christmas tree, the camera positioned in front of the television, a typical location for shooting toward the family's oft-seen dining room (the place where Sam often successfully entertains clients to make Darrin look good in front of Larry). Keith and his wife cross into the shot. Then, Sam moves screen right with Brockway's coat. As she turns, the camera crosses the axis, to a position that is unique in the history of the show. Now shot from behind the Christmas tree, Sam and Darrin share a tender kiss, accompanied by an orchestral version of "Silent Night." The camera cranes back, revealing the French doors at the back of the

Stephenses' home. While many scenes throughout the run of the show take place in the backyard (featuring hapless clients turned into cats and apes, Sam's gardening, the building of a gazebo), none has featured a camera position that shoots back into the house.

Aesthetically, *Bewitched,* shot telefilm style, is a repetitive show. However, repetition is the hallmark of all television: *All in the Family*'s proscenium set-ups of Archie's chair and *M*A*S*H*'s film style set-ups of the Swamp are just as repetitive. And yet the beauty of television is how it modulates such repetition, foregrounding minor shifts to achieve startling effects. This is as true of 1960s telefilm sitcoms as it is of those masterpieces of the "Television Renaissance."

I want to compare the final shot of "Sisters at Heart" to a similar moment in *Father Knows Best,* also shot telefilm style. In his History of Broadcasting course at the University of Texas at Austin, Tom Schatz offers an insightful analysis of a particular episode of this key transitional telefilm sitcom. In an episode featuring Robert Vaughn as a guest star love interest for Betty, Mr. Anderson speaks to his daughter as she prepares to go out on a date with Roger, a boy the popular people at school have assigned to her. Beekman (Vaughn) is too intellectual (he tries to get Betty to read Ralph Waldo Emerson's essay "Self-Reliance," but she refuses!) to pass muster with the leaders of the socially acceptable pack. Beekman beats Roger to the house, under the pretense of having forgotten his wallet there earlier in the day. In as complex a set-up as television has ever aired, Mr. Anderson sits deep into the set, in the living room. In the middle ground, Beekman turns from Betty as she answers the door to Roger. In a series of shot-reverse shots, Roger displays the exact unctuous behavior that Beekman predicted he would, presented to us visually under the auditory witness of both Mr. Anderson and Beekman.

As Beekman waves the Emerson book at Roger as he

leaves, the camera crosses the axis, revealing for the first time Beekman in the foreground, Mr. Anderson in the background, with the family's hearth as the backdrop of the set. In the normative proscenium shooting for *Father Knows Best's* era, the hearth's position would be the position of the cameras and the audience. However, the artists who made *Father Knows Best* find this moment, emphasizing Beekman and Mr. Anderson as both "right" for Betty, to trump all of the show's other efforts to mask its one-camera, out-of-continuity production technique.

In addition to hiding the fourth wall—in this case the hearth—of the set, the other major aesthetic element of the show is the laugh track. For without a live studio audience, the laugh track comes to serve as the technological replacement of television's aesthetic address of liveness.[7] I am not claiming that the end of "Sisters at Heart" is the artistic equivalent of this wonderful collapse of Emersonian idealism and 1950s conformity onto the aesthetics of multiple auditory positions that Schatz celebrates in this astonishing episode of *Father Knows Best*. However, I do want to use the example to demonstrate that the modulation of telefilm production techniques can and has produced such artistic flourishes.

Finally, as the discussion of the laugh tracks of 1960s telefilm sitcoms predicts, the one missing discussion in Barker's examination of telefilm aesthetics is the soundtrack. Quite simply, *Bewitched* features the most inventive, important soundtrack in the history of television. At the beginning of his seminal article, "Television/Sound," Rick Altman says, "With the exception of a few lucid pages by John Ellis, critics have systematically steered clear of TV sound, preferring instead to dwell on narrative, industrial, or image-oriented concerns. Yet a strong case can be made for the centrality of the sound track in the American commercial broadcast system" (39). Altman's primary reference point is *Dallas,* a show whose soundtrack pales in comparison to the aggressiveness of *Bewitched*'s.

Its wide range of cartoonish sounds that accompany the magical effects of its characters makes *Bewitched* aesthetically unique. The show is set apart from its live-action contemporaries in the sitcom universe, for example, *The Dick Van Dyke Show,* or the even more improbable *The Beverly Hillbillies* (CBS, 1962–71), by the use of synthesized or musical sound effects. Nearly every supernatural act, from conjuring objects, to teleportation, to summoning wind or other natural forces, is accompanied on the show by some kind of clang, chime, or other musical flourish.

The only worthy predecessor in this regard in the prime-time sitcom is *The Flintstones* (1960–65), also an ABC show of the early 1960s, which predated *Bewitched* by four seasons. In fact, that show, which always featured a set of auditory cues—for example, the sound of Fred and Barney's feet as they stopped their prehistoric car with no brakes— would engage the magic motif in its final sixth season, after the meteoric rise of *Bewitched* the season before. When the animated equivalents of Sam and Darrin appear in the episode "Samantha" (10/22/1965), Sam uses her magic to liberate Wilma and Betty from their prehistoric suburban drudgery, at least for one week.

This episode is worth discussing in some detail because it provides yet another example of telefilm's important yet neglected aesthetic role in the history of the American domestic sitcom. *The Flintstones,* as an animated show, can only be "shot" telefilm style. Adopted from the invention of classical film animation in Walt Disney shorts and features, animated narratives mimic one-camera film shooting, in which rotoscoping and other animation techniques provide simulated camera movements and cutting.

While the Hanna-Barbera company would become infamous for minimalist animation techniques (moving characters in front of static backgrounds), *The Flintstones* presented a domestic family sitcom that looked remarkably similar to its live-action equivalents. The show, of course, was a narrative reworking of *The Honeymooners,* focusing on Fred and Barney, the prehistoric versions of Ralph and Ed, who struggled to maintain patriarchal authority over their wives.

Like the "Samantha's Power Failure" and *I Love Lucy* "Job Switching" episodes analyzed earlier, the "Samantha" episode of *The Flintstones* offers a battle of the sexes plotline in which Fred and Barney state that their wives are not capable of going camping. Fred articulates this sexism most clearly, if tautologically: "Women just aren't equipped for the rigors of a rigorous existence." When Samantha and Darrin move into the neighborhood, and Darrin abandons Sam for the weekend to go boating with his buddy, Sam decides to help Wilma and Betty go camping near Fred and Barney to "show them we can do anything men can do, and better."

Fred and Barney overhear the women setting up camp, and confront them. In a simulation of proscenium shooting that is not that far from its live-action equivalent in "Samantha's Power Failure," a four-shot shows Fred, Wilma, Betty, and Barney together. This is then cut together with two-shots, one of the men and the other of the women. Sam serves as a mediating character, using her witchcraft to help the women triumph over the men. As with "Job Switching" and "Samantha's Power Failure," "Samantha" ends with the reinforcement of the status quo. Fred and Barney admit that "you're every bit as good as we are" and Sam analyzes this victory in middle-ground terms: "Congratulations, girls. You've struck a blow for togetherness" (and most definitely *not* for women's liberation!). When Fred and Barney inform the women that this togetherness will entail getting up at 5:00 a.m. to carry canoes up to a mountain lake, the women bow out, return home, and have tea.

The appearance of Sam and Darrin on *The Flintstones* is

a very early example of what Mimi White has called "cross-ing wavelengths." White analyzes the industrial importance of this intertextuality: "The promotional function of such in-terprogram referentiality supports viewership of the individ-ual programs by cross-fertilizing audiences. In this sense it localizes the general industry strategy of programming flow at the level of a specific episode" (53). Without question, this is the motor force behind ABC's economic method here. The episode does nothing to hide it. Early on, Wilma remarks: "I have the strangest feeling I've seen Samantha before." When Betty comments that Sam is "pretty enough to be in the movies or TV," Wilma produces a prehistoric promo for *Be-witched*: "That's who she looks like. The star of that wonder-ful witch TV show." However, there is more here than simply some industrial cross-promotion. Wilma looks directly into the "camera" (i.e., her animated face seems to stare directly at us in the audience) as she disavows the improbability of a modern 1960s witch showing up in prehistoric Bedrock: "Oh, but no. She wouldn't be living way out here in this neighborhood." The metatextual improbability of *Bewitched* suddenly haunts even *The Flintstones,* as the two texts' narra-tive methods are aligned.

While no episode of *Bewitched* ever featured such a di-rect example of "crossing wavelengths," *Bewitched* does in-herit from *The Flintstones* its cartoonish soundtrack, an ag-gressive series of comic sounds that enhance the aesthetic pleasures of the show. Interestingly, this "borrowing" of sound track aesthetics starts to go both ways with *Bewitched*'s success. One episode of *The Flintstones* later, "The Great Gazoo" (10/29/1965) introduces an alien (voiced by Harvey Korman) that only Fred and Barney can see, who appears with an aggressive percussion sound effect reminiscent of Endora's "pop in" on *Bewitched.*

Indeed, both *The Flintstones* and *Bewitched* would seem lifeless without their soundtracks that so seamlessly provide the flourishes of aural accompaniment. Altman captures this well when he argues that one of the functions of a television soundtrack is to "italicize" the image track: "Uniformly, [the sound] call[s] us to the image, to let us know that something is happening that we dare not miss; in short, something spectacular. The word is well chosen because it reveals the extent to which the italicizing function of sound serves to identify that which is worth looking at rather than just hearing" (46).

Bewitched's soundscape evolved over the eight-year run of the show, with the greatest experimentation occurring in season four, according to Bewitched fan Bill Lane ("Bewitched: Sounds of the Harp"). The only sound effect that is actually present for all eight seasons is Samantha's "nose twitch" tinkle, which is present in both the first and last episode and most every episode in between. Besides the twitch, hundreds of cartoonish sound effects were used to enhance the presentation of the magic special effects during the run of the show. One might expect so many odd sound effects to sound artificial or out of place; instead, the sound effects become quite "natural" within the conceit of the show. One "expects" the tinkle when Samantha twitches her nose, and it would not seem right if Endora "popped in" without her trademark chime. Indeed, the sound effects are a great part of what makes the show so attractive.

Even fans have remarked on the quality of the sound. In 2006, twenty-nine years after Bewitched left the air, the Internet site "Bewitched at Harpies Bizarre" has a suite of pages dedicated to the show's "sounds of the cosmos," including sound quizzes, sound bytes, and extensive listings of which sound effects are used in which episodes. Several sound effects in particular were staples on the show: the five-note "tinkle" accompanying Samantha's "nose twitch," and (in the last five seasons) the "harp swoosh" most often heard with the magical arm waves of witches and warlocks alike (http://www.harpiesbizarre.com).

Samantha's "twitch" is the most consistently used sound effect and likely the most well known. It accompanies Samantha's unique upper lip wiggle, which she usually uses to perform acts of magic. Although, in the pilot, her very earliest demonstrations of witchcraft are silent (there is no nose twitch and no sound effects as she proves to Darrin that she is a witch in their honeymoon suite), the nose twitch and accompanying five-note "tinkle" already make their appearance by late in this first episode. Here, as Samantha suffers through the excruciating dinner party with Darrin's snobbish ex-fiancée, Sheila, the urge to use a little magic becomes irresistible. Finally pushed to the breaking point, Samantha causes Sheila to sneeze forcefully, unzipping her evening gown. At this moment, the famous twitch is born.

The "harp-swoosh" is common in the later seasons (season 4 onward), and shows the playfulness of the show's creators in using sound. This sound effect was used in a number of situations where various magical characters use arm waves to perform magic, but is particularly innovative in the episode "Samantha's French Pastry" (#147, 11/14/68), in which the Emperor Napoleon is mistakenly summoned by Uncle Arthur. Paul Lynde's Arthur is comically over-the-top, and his wild gesticulations as he tries in vain to banish the French leader are reinforced by no less than eight successive harp-swooshes. This first attempt to return Napoleon fails, and Arthur finally realizes he needs to use "a little reverse English" to get the job done.

In this effect, Arthur does his "eight swoosh" incantation backward. The show's creators accomplish this by running the film backward. The sound is also run backward, setting up a scene that looks and sounds surprisingly like the famous dream sequence in *Twin Peaks* (ABC, 1990–91) where Agent Cooper encounters the "dancing dwarf." In creating the *Twin Peaks* effect, the creators made actor Michael J. Anderson recite his lines backward, resulting in the speech coming out eerily but mostly legibly (although the speech is also subtitled) when the film and soundtrack was run in reverse. In Arthur's backward Napoleon incantation, the speech does end up reverse (because it was filmed with Lynde speaking normally). Nonetheless, the *Twin Peaks* sequence was considered highly innovative at the time it aired, and yet *Bewitched* used the same technique more than twenty years earlier.

As with the image track, a world of repetition marks *Bewitched*'s soundtrack (we come to expect the sound of Samantha's nose twitch or Endora's pop in), but such norms set up opportunities for modulation. In "No Zip in My Zap" (#113, 10/12/67), Samantha's witchcraft goes on the fritz, eliciting a whole host of silly sounds as Samantha tries in vain to perform spells around the house. The laugh track follows Samantha's reaction, rather than the silly sounds, however. Thus, Samantha attempts a magic trick that fails to the tune of a cartoonish "sproing" sound, and Samantha grimaces. Only after the grimace do we hear the laugh (from the laugh track).

Entire episodes are built around aesthetic issues, particularly those involving the soundtrack. In "Samantha Loses Her Voice" (#150, 12/5/68), Uncle Arthur strikes again, this time inadvertently switching Samantha's and Darrin's voices. Each time Samantha speaks, she sounds like Darrin, and vice versa. This sets up a cascade where Uncle Arthur, Samantha, and Darrin end up exchanging voices in various ways throughout the episode.

The most frequent manipulation of the soundtrack involves magic pranks that cause Darrin to have to speak another language. In "Business, Italian Style" (#110, 9/21/67), Darrin has to learn Italian so that he can woo an Italian foods client for Larry. Endora is delighted that she and Sam will be able to go to an opera at La Scala until she realizes that Darrin is too dumb to learn another language. She casts a spell so that Darrin can speak perfect Italian, meaning well for a change, and so that her daughter can finally escape the "stultifying suburbs." The catch is that now Darrin can only speak perfect Italian, while his English is spoken with a stereotypical Italian accent, thus insulting his clients. Endora finally fixes her spell. With some quick thinking, Darrin explains that he was mocking the clients deliberately in order to explain the problems with cross-cultural advertising.

Similarly, in "Samantha and Darrin in Mexico City" (#170, 4/24/69), Darrin encounters more witchcraft-related linguistic troubles, leading up to one of the richest scenes, in terms of sound, of the entire show. Darrin is given the job of working on the Mexican Bueno soft drink account. Again, Darrin tries to take a record-based crash course, this time "So You Want to Speak Spanish Fluently in Five Minutes." Darrin has been working for hours, but when Endora pops in to speak to her daughter in Spanish, Darrin does not understand a word they say.

Crucially, the female witches are fluent in all the languages encountered on the show, while Darrin is hopeless in any foreign tongue, yet another case where Samantha's superior abilities frustrate her patriarchal husband. In the "Mexico City" episode, Endora casts a spell that allows him to speak perfect Spanish, but makes him disappear if he utters a word of English. When Darrin must make a presentation in both English and Spanish, the episode climaxes with a tour-de-force performance by Dick York who must rapidly switch between the two languages in the scene.

Sam helps Darrin get through the speech with an ingenious plan: He is to speak to one side of the room in Spanish. Then, he is to turn to the Americans, and Sam will cast a translation spell. Again demonstrating the modulation of telefilm visual aesthetics, the scene is set up with an expository long shot placed diagonally across the banquet table. The editor cuts into close-ups on Darrin as he speaks the various languages, Barker's claim that in 1960s telefilm, "close-ups were virtually never used" (170) notwithstanding. As Darrin gives his bilingual speech, the liberal sprinkling of five-note tinkles perfectly seasons the soundtrack as Sam casts one translation spell after another during Darrin's speech.

Finally, in an example of *Bewitched*'s modernism par excellence, "Out of Sync Out of Mind" (#116, 11/2/67) features a metatextual examination of the relationship between the image and soundtracks in a modern film production. The episode begins as a classic surveillance plot, with Darrin's parents coming for a surprise visit. With Phyllis and Frank's arrival imminent, Darrin shows home movies of Tabitha to Sam's Aunt Clara. Almost predictably, the tape-to-tape audio recorder and 8 mm film projector malfunction so that the sound and image fall out of synchronization. Trying to be helpful, Clara casts a spell: "Stop the voice until the picture is seen." It works, but not for the projection equipment; it is now Sam's voice and image that are out of sync.

Phyllis arrives, but without Frank. She reveals that she and Frank have been fighting and have separated. Darrin tries to help, but Phyllis refuses to even talk with Frank on the phone, thus matching the aesthetics of asynchronization with a thematic, marital version. Sam, making reference to the dominance of Italian postsynchronized dubbing of films, quips: "I feel like I'm in an Italian movie." While Dr. Bombay is able to cure Samantha, Clara mis-remembers her spell for getting rid of bad spells: it now causes Sam to break out in green stripes, resulting in the episode shifting from the aural to the visual as the threat that will reveal Sam's secret. At this point, Frank comes by and reconciles with Phyllis. However, the cycle of aural-visual crises in the Stephenses' household continues in the coda, as Darrin's voice goes out of sync, keeping him from meeting with his newly reconciled parents.

Regardless of plot circumstances, the *Bewitched* sound-scape is the aesthetic device that most expresses the show's interest in allegorizing the threat that public surveillance poses to the privacy of the characters. As mundane a sound as the Stephenses' doorbell plays a large part in the *Bewitched* soundscape, more so than any other American sitcom of which I am aware. The doorbell is a comfortingly domestic sound. It is familiar, a normal part of every household. The use of this sound bridges the Stephenses' household with our own. It invites us in, and asks us to enjoy this show about a suburban family perhaps much like our own. The door also represents the barrier between the mortal outside world and the magical world inside the Stephenses' home. When we are inside the home, we know relatives will pop in and, to the delight of children and adults alike, magical mayhem will ensue.

The sound of the doorbell also strikes at the heart of the comic tension of the show. Whereas in a nonsupernatural show the doorbell might bring visitors for a party or friends stopping by, in the Stephens household the door often brings unwanted intruders into the world of witchcraft. Nosy neighbor Gladys Kravitz comes to snoop on a regular basis, and Larry often drops by in a frenzy about the latest account. The doorbell announces only the arrival of mortals, who often inappropriately witness acts of magic, since, much to Darrin's chagrin, Endora or Serena can pop in completely unannounced. Witches do not require doorbells, or doors for that matter.

One can contrast *Bewitched* to its proscenium rival in the mid-1960s, *The Dick Van Dyke Show*. While the Petries clearly had a doorbell, and we heard it periodically, the Stephenses' doorbell rings incessantly throughout the show, as Larry, Mrs. Kravitz, and all of the others who threaten Sam's secret arrive at the most inopportune times, often just as one of Sam's relatives has created magical havoc in the household. While many domestic family sitcoms, including *The Dick Van Dyke Show,* rely on cutting back and forth between the husband's place of work (the comedy show in Rob's case) and home, in *Bewitched,* the plotlines are forced back to the Stephenses' household with a vengeance. Larry regularly brings clients over to Sam's space with little to no notice, so that she may woo the client into signing the ever-valuable contract. And thus, whether it announces Larry, Gladys Kravitz, or a door-to-door salesman, the doorbell serves as the first aural cue of the surveillance threat, and as such complements the visual use of the front doorway as a threshold between public and private that I have analyzed previously.

Identity Politics
and *Bewitched*

Bewitched was a popular television show that provided its viewers with 254 separate glimpses into the Stephenses' household over an eight-year time span. The show bridged an important cultural era, from the assassination of President Kennedy to the Nixon years, from civil rights struggles and the rise of second-wave feminism to free love and landing on the moon, and those real-life highs and lows could not help but filter into the ordinary suburban home (and its not-so-ordinary residents) at 1164 Morning Glory Circle. Because *Bewitched* witnessed so much cultural change in the time it was written and filmed, it provides a particularly fertile ground for understanding the cultural currents that flowed through 1960s U.S. society. Reducing *Bewitched*'s textual systems to a pithy summary robs the show of, among other things, its potentially important status as a collection of cultural historical documents that uncompromisingly negotiate the political climate surrounding it. I first want to investigate the ways in which *Bewitched* as a cultural historical document grapples specifically with the changing identity politics of the 1960s.

Dana Heller contends that a "fragmentation" of the family occurred in America after World War II, which in turn resulted in a shift in popular culture's representations of the family. She labels the representations of the family that develop after World War II "post-family romances," and sees these texts as reactions to the prewar Freudian family romances. Heller specifically links the shift in the family romance to postwar developments in the politics of identity: "The post-family romance emerges in American culture as early as the mid-1950s when postwar promises of domestic unity began to degenerate with the emergence of an African-American civil rights movement, demographic changes in the American workplace, and the increasing articulation of American middle-class women's discontent with the intensified structuring of their domestic roles" (7). Heller uses three social crises to define the post-family romance: the conflicts over race, class, and gender. In this and the next two sections, I will investigate *Bewitched* as a show about the post-family romance in its negotiation of these three social crises, beginning with the show's intersection with racism.

Sylvia Moss identifies "the comedy of in-group and out-group" and notes that *Bewitched* is one example of this type of comedy, arguing that the show's humor is built around conflicts between social outcasts, the out-groups ("this small, alien culture"), and the "normal" Americans, the in-groups ("modern society"). Although Samantha, as a witch in a mortal world, clearly belongs to an out-group, *Bewitched* refuses to firmly situate the specific reasons for Samantha's out-group status. In separate episodes, it is intimated that her "deviance" from the modern society represented by Darrin has to do with, variously, racial, class-based, and/or gender identity.

In one collection of episodes, *Bewitched* represents Samantha and Darrin's marriage as "mixed," that is, multiracial. The best example of this is the two-episode season opener of the crucial seventh-season plotline involving the Stephenses' visit to Salem, "To Go or Not to Go, That Is the Question" (#201, 9/24/70) and "Salem, Here We Come (#202, 10/1/70). Those episodes directly invoke the mixed marriage metaphor as Hepzibah, the queen of the witches, comes to visit the Stephenses' house to determine whether the mixed marriage needs to be dissolved. As a result of her close observation of Darrin's life, she ends up falling in love with airline magnate Ernest Hitchcock (Cesar Romero), one of Darrin's clients, and decides that mortals are not as bad as she once believed. In this case, the witch bias against mortals is cured in typically liberal fashion: love proves stronger than hate. However, numerous episodes are devoted to mortals' biases against witches, with Samantha being discriminated against because of her different heritage.

The Halloween episodes in particular represent witches as an oppressed minority group suffering unfair stereotypical imaging from the in-group. The direct invocation of the civil rights movement's protest strategies is found in the episode, "The Witches Are Out." The witches fight against their popular image as ugly old crones, much as simultaneous NAACP protests against *Amos 'n' Andy* (CBS, 1951–53) for peddling stereotypes of black men as lazy and shiftless resulted in the show being quietly removed from syndication by CBS.

The second season's Halloween episode again returns to the theme of witch stereotyping. In "Trick or Treat" (#43, 10/28/65), Endora, upset that Darrin forced Samantha to miss a Halloween party so she could entertain his clients at their home, turns Darrin into a werewolf. When Darrin is forced to hide in the closet for fear of exposing his otherness to his client, Sam accuses Endora of being a witch in the stereotypical, discriminatory mortal sense of the word. The show hereby engages a very crucial point about stereotyping: that minorities taking the bait and living up to the lies and partial truths told about them is exactly the response on which the bigots rely. This logic convinces Endora, who then apologizes to Darrin. Although this is a rare occurrence in the show (as is Darrin apologizing to Endora), it happens frequently enough to be a noteworthy feature of *Bewitched*'s peculiar take on the family romance.

While *Bewitched*'s in-group/out-group allegorization of the family romance, as represented most clearly in its Halloween episodes, points to a progressive, nuanced engagement with the civil rights struggles of the 1960s, it would be a mistake to reduce the show to this one engagement with racial politics. Driven by the cold war liberal attitudes of its creators, director William Asher and his wife, Elizabeth Montgomery, *Bewitched* often engages in the transparent practices of paternalistic, centrist racial politics. Several episodes feature the witches' use of their powers to magically correct (specifically African American) racial injustices.

As mentioned, one of the show's most celebrated episodes, "Sisters at Heart," presents a feel-good Christmas message of racial tolerance. In the episode, Darrin's racist client, Mr. Brockway, pulls his account from McMann and Tate when he mistakenly assumes that Tabitha's black friend Lisa is Darrin's daughter and concludes that Darrin is in a "mixed marriage." Developed from a story idea submitted by an English class at the inner-city Thomas Jefferson High School in Los Angeles, "Sisters at Heart" is indicative of the shortcomings of liberal race ideology. Criticism of such ideology has long been leveled at such films as *The Defiant Ones* (Stanley Kramer, 1958) and *Guess Who's Coming to Dinner* (1967). In the former film—about two prison escapees, one black and one white, who are chained together—a virulent racist (Tony Curtis) is quickly cured of his disease, and the narrative ends in the warm sumptuousness of familial togetherness: Sidney Poitier hugs Curtis as the sheriff arrives to take them both back to prison. Similarly, in "Sisters at Heart," Mr. Brockway basks in the glow of the Stephenses' holiday living room, sitting down at the dinner table to eat a meal of "integrated turkey . . . white meat and dark." This meal is reminiscent of the ending of *Guess Who's Coming to Dinner*, in which Spencer Tracy famously gives his blessing to his daughter's marriage to Sidney Poitier. With Tracy's speech, the film implies that only white patriarchs have the cultural authority to declare that racism is wrong. Once Tracy speaks, all racial problems are considered solved. Tracy's spectacular monologue at the end of the film is mirrored in Brockway's magically found soft-heartedness at the end of the *Bewitched* episode.

This paternalistic approach to liberal racial tolerance (black characters are portrayed as impossibly perfect, and interracial relationships are "approved" by "forward-thinking" white folks) is best expressed in *Bewitched* through Samantha's self-appointed role as the good citizen. In numerous episodes, Samantha takes it upon herself to right social injustice, even if it involves ignoring Darrin's prohibitions against using witchcraft. Often, these episodes involve repetitions of the basic grammar of the sitcom. Samantha lobbies for a new traffic light in "Eye of the Beholder," a plot that perpetually returns, most recently as Homer Simpson becomes Springfield's safety officer in an equally foundational episode of *The Simpsons* (#3, "Homer's Odyssey," 1/21/90). In another *Bewitched* episode, "Samantha Twitches for UNICEF" (#166, 3/27/69), Samantha uses her powers to convince a businessman under the mortal spell of a greedy gold digger to make good on his $10,000 pledge to UNICEF. In yet another, "Samantha Fights City Hall" (#149, 11/28/68), she uses her witchcraft to make a developer change his mind about converting a beloved city park into a shopping mall. In "Splitsville" (#140, 5/16/68), Samantha even protects domes-

tic morality. In an odd reversal, Samantha spies on perenni-
ally nosy neighbor Gladys Kravitz—out on the street after
she has chosen to leave her husband Abner—and takes it
upon herself to mend the marriage.

As discussed earlier, Samantha's good citizenship is devoted to leveling the playing field for African Americans in
"Samantha at the Keyboard," in which Endora zaps Tabitha
into a piano virtuoso after losing patience with her toddler-
like keyboard tinkling. When Sam's delighted piano teacher
insists on taking Tabitha on a world tour, Samantha uses
witchcraft to find a nonmagical prodigy whom she can use to
take attention off Tabitha. She discovers one in a public
school, a boy named Matthew Williams, the son of the
school's African American janitor. Because the family cannot
afford a piano, Matthew has been forced to practice at the
school while his father sweeps up. Sam gets Mr. Monroe his
prodigy, and is able to start the career of a promising African
American pianist in a culture in which he would never have
had the opportunity to be heard otherwise.

While liberal in its sensibilities toward African Americans, *Bewitched* nonetheless engages in racist representational strategies. In "A Majority of Two" (#136, 4/11/68),
Darrin's client Kensu Mishimoto (played by a white actor,
Richard Haydn) falls in love with Samantha's Aunt Clara.
Knowing that Aunt Clara's unreliable magic will expose their
family secret, Samantha uses Clara's warlock boyfriend Ocky
to forestall Mishimoto's proposal of marriage to Clara. The
embarrassed and hurt Mishimoto pulls his account from Mc-
Mann and Tate and attempts to leave the country in disgrace,
having "lost face" with his business associates. Samantha
then intervenes magically, convincing Mishimoto that his
sudden exit has caused her to also lose face. Glance object
cuts and special effects reveal that when Mishimoto looks at
her, he can only see a cloudy blank on Samantha's face. After
magically arranging a "chance" encounter with a young

Japanese beauty with whom Mishimoto can fall in love, the Japanese businessman decides that Samantha is right and he should stay and complete his business in New York.

The plot begins with the startling possibility of the interracial relationship between Mishimoto and Clara—highly culturally significant because the episode was broadcast a mere ten months after the Supreme Court finally struck down the U.S. Southern states' shameful antimiscegenation laws in the wonderfully named *Loving v. Virginia* case (6/12/67). However, the show ends conventionally, finding a Japanese woman for Mishimoto. In sum, the show represents cultural differences in international business in the most baldly stereotypical fashion (at one point Larry gushes to Sam, "You really know your Orientals!"), without even having the good sense to use a Japanese actor to play a Japanese businessman.

The representation of racial difference in *Bewitched* runs the gamut from provocative critiques of U.S. racism to endorsements of abject discrimination. Weighed together, *Bewitched* generally features a liberal approach to race based on tolerance. In some episodes' liberal approach to race, Lynn Spigel is correct when she asserts that "fantastic hyperbolic representations of cultural difference took the place of the more 'realistic' portrayals. At a time when the civil rights movement had gained ground, these programs dramatized the exclusionary practices of the middle-class suburbs, not in realistic ways, but through exaggerated, comedic representations" (220). In many ways, this analysis is an astute critique of the escapist dimensions of *Bewitched.* The allegorization of in-group/out-group tensions avoids the realities of discrimination against racial minorities in the 1960s. Simultaneously, *Bewitched*'s liberal imperative also engaged quite directly with discrimination. Never quite able to escape its political centrism, the show uses magic to paper over the depths of the problems of white supremacy, arguing that a gentle nudge, whether magical or not hardly seems to matter, would turn any racist into an upstanding member of the community.

An Aristocracy of Witches: Class Politics in *Bewitched*

Even considering only the episodes foregrounding racial difference, *Bewitched* cannot be reduced to one formulaic resolution of the politics of in-group/out-group tensions. Issues of class are also crucial to understanding the show's varying approaches to identity politics. Samantha's family is clearly aristocratic: both of her parents, played by the theatrically trained Agnes Moorehead and Maurice Evans, project an aura of formal elegance. One marker of this elegance is the theater itself. In "Samantha's Good News," Endora attempts to make Maurice jealous because she discovers he is having an affair with a young witch. Endora in turn begins dating John Van Millwood (Murray Matheson), a Shakespearean actor. To vie for Endora, John and Maurice engage in an acting contest, not with the low cultural material of the domestic family sitcom, but with Shakespearean recitations. In the end, Endora chooses Maurice and harmony is restored in time for Samantha's announcement that she is having a second baby.

The episode "Samantha's Super Maid" (#154, 1/2/69) also plays with the tensions of aristocracy meeting the bourgeoisie. Samantha's mother-in-law, Mrs. Stephens, forces her to hire a maid. Witches can do household chores with a wave of their hand, and thus the concept of work, as with aristocrats, has little meaning. Having the power to have someone else (in this case, magic) do the cleaning clearly aligns Samantha with the aristocracy. However, Samantha, much to her parents' horror, enjoys—or at least is forced by the 1960s scriptwriters to insist that she does—doing housework the mortal way, which codes Sam as a "normal" American housewife. By episode's end, Sam has, with a little magic, arranged for the maid to go work for a "real" aristocratic family, protecting the secret of the magical household for another week.

In a follow-up episode, "Samantha's Yoo-Hoo Maid" (#172, 9/25/69), the threat of mortals witnessing Samantha's secret power is solved when, this time at Endora's urging, the witch Esmeralda comes to help Samantha as both maid and babysitter. However, Esmeralda's occult antics nearly lose Darrin an important account, and it is agreed that, due to the necessity of keeping up mortal appearances, Esmeralda can only come to the household for occasional babysitting. That the aristocratic Samantha chooses to adopt Darrin's bourgeois lifestyle, and thus live without magic or maid, is an ambiguous political act. On the one hand, she is subsuming her heritage in favor of her husband's; yet on the other hand, her decision to reject that heritage is a critique of Endora's and Maurice's smug aristocratic superiority.

Other episodes reveal this class-bound smugness as a feature of bourgeois culture itself, not just as the domain of aristocrats. In "The Battle of Burning Oak" (#164, 3/13/69), Darrin attempts to solidify his upward mobility by joining a country club. While Endora shows her disgust for the conceited men in the club by turning Darrin into a similar snob, Samantha must pass muster with the women of the admissions committee. When Samantha becomes horrified at the prideful class pretensions of the club wives, she uses her powers to unearth the secret family histories of some prominent members of the club. For example, one person's ancestor did indeed come over on the Mayflower, as he likes to brag, but not as an upstanding Pilgrim: he was a stowaway, the witches' research reveals. Sam's interventions cause the club to change its admissions rules.

To emphasize Samantha's democratic victory over an exclusive country club is not to argue for the show's inherent progressivism. While *Bewitched* generally articulates a centrist liberal disdain for injustice, it also suffers from the contradictions of that very same centrism, the constitutive feature of cold war liberal politics. "Soap Box Derby" (#90, 12/29/66) exists somewhere else on the class-based political continuum. Whereas "Samantha's Super Maid" and "Samantha's Yoo-Hoo Maid" are primarily concerned with social class issues as expressed within the dynamics of the family, "The Battle of Burning Oak" and "Soap Box Derby" constitute episodes in which Samantha engages in a form of public citizenship, attempting to right social injustices. In "The Battle of Burning Oak," she succeeds in ridiculing the classist assumptions of mortal high society. However, in "Soap Box Derby," she operates in a way that bludgeons the working class with her own bourgeois morality.

As in a number of the episodes of the show—in "Little Pitchers Have Big Fears" (#6, 10/22/64), she helps a neighborhood boy gain confidence in playing baseball—Samantha befriends a young boy, Johnny Mills, and helps him prepare a soap box racer because Johnny's father, a working-class mechanic, is too busy with his work to help his son. Trouble brews when busybody neighbor Gladys Kravitz, whose nephew is beaten by Johnny in the race, suspects Samantha of foul play and calls for a judicial hearing on the race results. Samantha finally convinces Mr. Mills to come and support his son, which he does to help his son defend himself against Mrs. Kravitz's unjust charges. The episode ends with support for Samantha's meddling, arguing that her middle-class assumptions about parenting are the correct ones for the raising of the boy, class pressures on the father be damned. If Samantha can find the time to help the boy, then so can his father, regardless of his work responsibilities and her access to witchcraft.

In constructing this typology of the show's different episodes, I am suggesting that the show specifically *does not* construct a stable stance regarding issues of race, class, and gender. In "The Battle of Burning Oak," Samantha fights discriminatory class assumptions, but in "Soap Box Derby," she enforces them. In the race episodes discussed earlier ("Samantha at the Keyboard," "Sisters at Heart"), the show calls for an end to racism, but also posits white Samantha as the benefactor and protector of black people. This work reveals that *Bewitched* is the articulation of a set of historical contradictions that, as with the culture it emerges from, is deeply conflicted about such matters.

As both a matter of social class and gender, *Bewitched* is also often concerned with the instability of Darrin's job in light of Samantha's ability to perform his advertising work as well as the work she has been assigned at home. Samantha's talent at coming up with advertising slogans is not necessarily a result of her witchcraft either. As I describe below, Samantha regularly comes up with good ideas from the (albeit wacky, witchcraft-induced) situations in which Sam, Darrin, and his clients find themselves. In terms of social class, the show is at its most subversive when it ridicules the basic notions of Darrin's advertising career. Interestingly, unlike subsequent "quality television," such as *The Mary Tyler Moore Show,* in which feminist issues would be articulated via a "workplace" family, *Bewitched* maintains the classic structure of a traditional domestic family sitcom such as *Father Knows Best* (in which the husband works and then returns home to the domestic space where most of the show takes place) even as it activates the feminist tensions of talented woman versus stay-at-home wife.

In contrast to *Father Knows Best, Bewitched* takes place almost as much in Darrin's office as in the home. In this way, *Bewitched* offers a prototype for quality television via an elegant blending of the two spaces, corporate and domestic.

87

However, whereas the critique of the absurdity of the workplace is muted in *The Mary Tyler Moore Show*—while Ted Baxter is indeed a buffoon, Mr. Grant and the others are consummate, if flawed, professionals—*Bewitched*'s critique of Darrin's corporate identity is relentless. In the largest grouping of episodes, Darrin's career in advertising is threatened by Samantha's magical relatives. While it is this plotline that previous *Bewitched* criticism has offered as the "prototypical" episode trajectory, it is important to note that less than one-third of the episodes actually involve this type of story. These episodes also connect *Bewitched* to the larger postwar film culture, in which the nature of U.S. capitalism was put on trial in films such as *The Man in the Gray Flannel Suit* (Nunnally Johnson, 1957). Such serious obsessions would gradually morph into comedy by the 1960s. Jack Boozer asserts that *How to Succeed in Business without Really Trying* (David Swift, 1967) served "to demonstrate just how conformist and ludicrous the world of business can be" (12), but this is something that *Bewitched* had been doing for three previous seasons.

In each of the "career" episodes, witchcraft, either the result of a purposeful or accidental spell, has placed Darrin in a position in which he is about to lose an important account. Since Larry either threatens to or actually does fire Darrin in nearly every instance that a client voices disapproval, Darrin's job, and thus the family's control over the safe domain of domestic suburbia, is constantly threatened by this magical interference. Yet Samantha invariably uses her wit, not her magic, to invent a catchy advertising slogan that simultaneously preserves the family secret and lands Darrin the account.

The best early example of this is the "Ho Ho the Clown" episode in which Samantha has to think fast to assuage an enraged toy-company client who suspects nepotism when Tabitha wins an on-air contest (due to Endora's prideful interference in her granddaughter's life). Sam twitches up a "Tabitha doll" and convinces the client it was all a publicity stunt for a new toy. In another episode, the appearance of Leonardo da Vinci (#124, "Samantha's da Vinci Dilemma," 12/28/67) leads Sam to come up with an idea for "tooth paint" for children. In "This Little Piggie" (#220, 2/25/71) Samantha has to convince a client that Darrin's hogshead (Endora thought he was pig-headed) is just an innovative way to sell sausage. Sam similarly explains that the appearance of Paul Revere (played by perennial game show host Bert Convy) in "Paul Revere Rides Again" (#206, 10/29/70) is a stunt to convince a British textile importer to use the slogan "The British are coming."

"Going Ape" (#162, 2/27/69) features Samantha doing more fast thinking to explain a cologne model who tears up a TV studio (he was really a chimp that Tabitha turned into a man). Significantly, in this particular episode Samantha has to save Darrin's career even though Darrin is not even in the episode. This was one of the many episodes of season 5 that needed to be filmed without Dick York, who was dealing with an increasingly debilitating chronic back injury. This episode is a prime example of how industrial pressures produced a shift in the textual system, with Samantha having to play off Larry rather than Darrin to keep the premise of the show intact.

Interestingly, when witchcraft is used to make up a slogan, the results are disastrous. In "If the Shoe Pinches" (#197, 3/26/70), Endora has a leprechaun annoy Darrin so much that he wastes the entire Saturday that he was supposed to use to create a campaign to sell peaches. Furious, Samantha forces Endora to magically help Darrin come up with a slogan at the last minute. The resulting slogan— "Don't shave the fuzz off of your peaches, let Barber do it"— is so awful that Endora has to zap the client into liking it. At episode's end, Sam reminds Endora that she will need to zap the whole world to have the slogan succeed. Similarly, in "Man of the Year" (#139, 5/2/68), Endora has enchanted Darrin so that all his clients will love even his least creative ideas. Even when the spell is removed, Darrin cannot get the clients to consider his better ideas, and in the end he has to have Samantha temporarily zap the clients one last time to prevent their ruin through disastrous ad campaigns.

Bewitched continuously undermines Samantha's stated desire to live the mortal life, making the antifeminist politics of the show ambiguous at best. In "Samantha and the Troll" (#219, 2/18/71), Sam leaves her cousin Serena in charge of the household so that she can go see Dr. Bombay for her "10,000-spell checkup," a notion that shatters a conservative reading of the show: if Samantha truly meant to render herself completely subservient to Darrin's wishes to not do witchcraft and maintain the home "in the normal, mortal way," then she certainly should not need a checkup of her magical abilities after thousands of spells.

Similarly, Darrin's patriarchal imperative, his control over a rising career on Madison Avenue, is regularly under siege by the interventions of Samantha's family. In this way, the show is about the feminine threat posed to the male-dominated economy. This is a profound reversal from typical twentieth-century vilifications of mass culture as feminine. Instead, Larry Tate, Darrin's boss, in episode after episode, is lampooned as the capitalist who will say and sell anything in order to make money. Larry is indeed a comic foil for everything capitalistic. He is an atrocious yes-man to clients, contradicting himself at every turn to agree with everything they might say. This quality is especially notable when he has been bewitched. For example, in "And Something Makes Four" (#175, 10/16/69), Maurice's spell to make everyone adore the Stephenses' newborn son Adam has a typically consumerist effect on Larry. Upon seeing the boy, Larry immediately insists on making him the new face for a baby food label being represented by McMann and Tate. When Endora appeals to Maurice's haughty aristocratic bearing and convinces him to remove the spell, Larry's plan is foiled, saving Adam from exploitation by mere mortals.

Besides ridiculing Larry, the show offers a coherent and compelling critique of the dangers of excess consumerism. In "Samantha's da Vinci Dilemma," Leonardo, accidentally zapped into the Stephenses' home by Aunt Clara, is horrified to find Darrin using a parody of the *Mona Lisa* to sell toothpaste. Only Sam's suggestion to jettison the crass use of the famous painting in favor of a palette of tooth paints bearing an image of da Vinci himself saves the day. This episode certainly critiques the world of advertising, where everything is for sale.

Finally, with regard to social class and its relationship to Darrin's career, the show mostly desires to produce a liberal critique of materialism. In "Charlie Harper, Winner" (#99, 3/2/67), Samantha meets an old college friend of Darrin's, Charlie Harper, and his wife, Daphne. When Charlie and Daphne brag incessantly about how rich and successful they are, Samantha retaliates (again returning to the basic premise of the series pilot when Sam used witchcraft to embarrass a snooty ex-girlfriend of Darrin's), zapping up a mink coat but passing it off as a gift from Darrin. Darrin flies into a rage at Sam's fling with crass materialism, leading a remorseful Sam to declare that while mink coats will come and go, there is only one Darrin Stephens. When Daphne indicates that she would still do anything for that coat, Charlie realizes—as do we in the audience—that what Sam and Darrin have is priceless, and cannot be made, even by magic.

The show's critique of such materialism extends beyond this feel-good paean to true love. Despite the reaffirmation of Darrin and Sam's domestic bliss that closes every episode, Darrin's position as the family's economic provider is not only threatened by Samantha's ability to zap up anything she may desire, but also by the show's regular under-mining of the whole business culture. Advertising is often portrayed as crass, and Larry is a comically over-the-top huckster. Most intriguingly, Samantha, even without witch-craft, turns out to be much better at the advertising game than Darrin. The subversive undercurrent of the show is that money, material goods, and advertising are aspects of human culture that are absurd to the witches, who can manipulate time and space and have instant access to anything they de-sire.

Love the House, Hate the Work: *Bewitched* and Feminism

Bewitched criticism has thoroughly assessed the gendered component of the domestic versus workplace conflict. As with the race and class issues, the political implications of the show's grappling with gender roles is fundamentally ambigu-ous, as evidenced in the opposing stances on these issues by different academic critics. In the show, Samantha demon-strates significant discontent with the domestic role she is as-signed, not in her outward dialogue, but in her actions. For despite her promises to abstain from witchcraft, she often "twitches" to do housework rather than doing it the "mortal" way (i.e., the way all American housekeepers, who happen to mostly be women, are forced to, through tedious labor). Yet nearly every episode ends with Samantha endorsing Darrin's patriarchal dominance as appropriate for her.

This polysemy—the short-term episodic plots endorse patriarchy while the long-term stakes of the serial narrative endorse feminist discontent with patriarchy—is what Dana Heller's approach to popular culture, as articulated in the concept of the post-family romance, brings into view. In

Darrin's home is most definitely not his castle, in "Long Live the Queen" (9/7/67).

terms of a feminist position, Heller contends that family romances "need to be read as fields of competition or as stages on which feminism may be said to compete for the spotlight along with numerous other performers or kinds of discourse" (10). This struggle between discourses and political sensibilities is evident when multiple episodes of *Bewitched* are juxtaposed.

The most obvious, and most discussed, episodes in the *Bewitched* typology are those that deal with Samantha's contradictory position as a witch and a housewife. The academic critical debate around *Bewitched* has almost exclusively centered on the show's gender politics, arguing over whether or not the character of Samantha is a progressive gender representation. This work results in two diametrically opposed readings of *Bewitched*, and critics are almost evenly split as to whether the show represents a progressive or conservative representation of gender.

The argument for the show's conservative nature with respect to gender usually focuses on each episode's ending. Samantha and her family are positioned as the gender troublemakers who throw Darrin's patriarchal control into question, a control that is restored each week as Samantha resubscribes to the legitimacy of Darrin's power. Of the seven major academic essays about *Bewitched,* three of the authors (Darrell Hamamoto, David Marc, and Gerald Jones) view the show as articulating this conservative message: Hamamoto claims that the show is about, "The control of transgressions against a normative social order based on male dominance" (63), but does not offer any specific episode of *Bewitched* as evidence for his analysis. Marc argues for *Bewitched*'s conservative ideological position, seeing Darrin Stephens as "the most ideologically committed sexist of them all" (135). Marc further argues that Darrin enforces a "puritanical order" (134), without ever considering the fairly large beating that Puritan repression takes in the "return-to-Salem" episodes.

As for Samantha, Marc reads her as a suffocating, ideological stooge ("Sam professes to agree with Darrin that what is normal is indeed proper: the status quo as platonic ideal. . . . A rare and extraordinary being living in a colony of conformist slugs, Samantha can develop no real ties to her 'normal' neighbors" [136–37]), relying on just episode two, "Be It Ever So Mortgaged." Jones continues this positioning of Samantha as cultural dupe, claiming that she "personified mass culture's ideal wife, in that last moment before mass culture tried to encompass the woman's movement" (177). Jones makes no bones about what he thinks of the show: "*Bewitched* was as anti-feminist, anti-sexual, and pro-centrist as a sit-com could be" (177). Importantly, Jones does open up the possibility of ideological contradictions—"It was also, however, peculiarly ineffective in selling its own point of view"—although he does not explore this assertion in any detail.

In contrast, Susan Douglas has been the strongest feminist defender of *Bewitched* and other 1960s "magicoms," such as *I Dream of Jeannie*.[8] Douglas positions *Bewitched's* gender politics within the contradictions of the Kennedy administration, the same cold war liberalism that fueled Asher and Montgomery as they crafted the show in the first place. On the one hand, Douglas observes that Kennedy was a conventional sexist: "Journalist May Craig stood up and asked the president what he was doing for women. Kennedy quipped that he was sure that, whatever it was, it wasn't enough, implying that women were never satisfied, and shared a big laugh with the predominantly male press corps" (124). On the other hand, President Kennedy established the Presidential Commission on the Status of Women with Eleanor Roosevelt as chair. In this climate, Douglas alleges, *Bewitched* emerged as a show that she positions on the side of Kennedy, the supporter of Roosevelt: "It is easy to dismiss *Bewitched* as one of the dumbest and kitschiest shows ever produced, but it would be a mistake to do so. . . . It was one of the few shows with an appealing female lead character who offered female viewers a respite from, as well as a critique of, male domination" (127). Scholars wishing to highlight *Bewitched's* gender progressiveness in this way—its opening up of gender contradictions—focus on the long-term plot of the show, but only insofar as it continually perpetuates a repetitive second act. In this argument, Samantha's rupture of Darrin's patriarchal control is seen to forever continue, being temporarily resolved in one episode but then immediately reactivated in the first minutes of the next.

Recent *Bewitched* criticism has been more forthcoming about the political challenges the show offers. Lynn Spigel contends that *Bewitched* critiques the very form of the sitcom itself: "Programs like *Bewitched* . . . poked fun at narrative conventions of the sit-com form and engaged viewers in a popular dialogue through which they might reconsider social ideals" (214). Barry Putterman continues arguing for *Bewitched*'s progressiveness in relation to this critique of the sitcom form itself by examining the show's relationship to advertising:

> It is of paramount importance to this show that all aspects of Darrin's emotional tightrope act converge at the point of his job in the advertising industry. For *Bewitched* tells us that maintaining a non-threatening and friendly rapport with the public and persuading other people to accept your own point-of-view without seeming to have pushed them into it—in short, advertising—is what the new era is all about. (98)

What the critics in the *Bewitched*-as-conservative camp use as evidence—Darrin's ability to convince Samantha of the benefits of "normal" suburban living—becomes, in Putterman's analysis, exactly what the show is seen to be parodying and "making strange." Dana Heller continues this critical tradition, positioning *Bewitched* as an "auto-critique" of the 1950s sitcom: "[*Bewitched*] provided an auto-critique—something TV has mastered over the decades—on network packaging and marketing of the American Dream represented by the socially insipid Cleavers and Nelsons" (54).

The totality of the *Bewitched* episodes I have examined reveal large rifts in the ideological fabric of 1960s American culture. Sam's ability to influence the flow of time in "Samantha's Old Man," where she projects both herself and Darrin into the future so that he can see their lives together as an elderly couple, reveals a superhuman power that clearly threatens the logic of a patriarchy insistent on the scientific control of time and lineage. Yet, as discussed earlier, when one sees the viciousness of Darrin's patriarchal presence in the "driving" episodes ("Driving Is the Only Way to Fly," "Open the Door Witchcraft"), one becomes hard pressed to

argue for the show's progressiveness. Because of such dis-
parate episodes, a politically inclined criticism of a television
series that focuses on just a few episodes—as has *Bewitched*'s
gender-oriented analyses—is less useful than it should be,
since there are episodes that support either perspective.

One of the smartest reviews of *Bewitched*'s complexity
comes not out of academic criticism but from a *TV Guide* article written by Isaac Asimov during the show's run. Asimov
cunningly captures the complications of the show's political
stance by feigning an argument between himself (as a conservative patriarch) and his daughter (representing liberated
womanhood). Mockingly titled, "Husbands, Beware!" Asimov's review warns his male readers that a huge shift has occurred in the television landscape between the times of *I Love
Lucy* and *Bewitched*: "On each occasion [of *I Love Lucy*], Lucy
was absolutely terrified of her husband finding out . . . [Yet
on *Bewitched*]: How can I bring myself to tell you the mind-
shattering nature of the result? The husband is terrified"
(10). The Asimov persona whose sexist opinions are represented in the review argues that *Bewitched* is "a monstrous
production that is destroying all that is most holy and wonderful in the husband-wife relationship because it is representing a woman who is in control of the situations around
her, and a husband who is patently not in control of them"
(10).

Further complicating the politics of the review itself,
Asimov introduces another interpreter of the show: his
daughter. She, conversely, sees the history of the television
sitcom as patently sexist: "But Daddy, don't you see that Lucy,
Gladys, Joan, She and all the rest always get their way? Don't
you see they have to wheedle and connive to get it? It's dis-
graceful. It makes women out to be creatures without dignity
or self-respect and destroys them as people" (8). She argues
that *Bewitched* is thoroughly in keeping with this sexist trajectory: "Don't you see that *Bewitched* is just another exam-

ple of the degradation of womanhood? Here's a woman with unimaginable power and she uses it to shore up her husband's ego, make him look good, help him keep his job, beat down his enemies. Has she no life of her own?" (10). This 1969 tongue-in-cheek review of the show, penned five years before the birth of academic television criticism and fifteen years before the rise of feminist analysis of television, accurately foreshadows the coming debate about *Bewitched*'s gender politics.

The ambiguities of the Asimovs' review are as intriguing as its strategy. The way Asimov concludes the review serves as a clarification of this: "One thing I am going to do at once is to keep my own wife in a state of wholesome terror . . . and I am going to do it right now!—Or maybe tomorrow. Anyway, I'm definitely going to do it sometime this week or possibly next, if I can catch her in a good humor" (10). While clearly parodying the patriarchal husband with his threat to keep his wife in line where she belongs, the ending is also a winking nod at another truism of patriarchy: that while men control things on the surface, underneath it is their wives who run the show. Where the irony ends and a hidden "truth" is revealed may in fact be where the patriarchal affirmation implicit in the piece arises. Regardless of what we may conclude about the politics of the review, its assault on the reductive progressive-versus-conservative argument about *Bewitched* is well taken.

Starting with this foundation of feminist criticism, I want my methodology of exploring *Bewitched* to illuminate issues of gender in ways that an exclusively feminist focus has not been able to reveal. As it turns out, this strategy often leads directly back to issues of gender. For example, shifting away from arguments about Samantha as a representation of Woman can lead toward considering her role as a time-traveler. Of particular importance here is the much heralded (in the popular discourse about the show, but not touched on in academic criticism) seventh season trip to seventeenth-century Salem where Samantha confronts the illogic of the Salem witch trials. Here, the time travel analysis returns us squarely back to the realm of gender issues, as the show is deliberate in its representation of the gendered components of the Puritan persecution of the witches: the judges are all male, while Samantha eloquently argues the case for the witches to these angry men.

The Politics of History in *Bewitched*

If identity politics in general, and gender politics in particular, is not the sole focus of *Bewitched,* it remains to be established what other themes the show's textual strategies engage. Thus far, I have discussed episodes dealing with race, class, and gender, but what remains is the most interesting of *Bewitched*'s textual strategies: the episodes dealing with the magical manipulation of history. *Bewitched* is such a complicated textual system because it investigates history in its traditional sense while also exploring the show's very own history as a representational system. While there are famous modernist films that explore such issues, such as *Last Year at Marienbad* (Alain Resnais, 1959), the notion that a popular sitcom would perform work exploring history and memory remains unconsidered.

Generally, history impinges on *Bewitched* in two ways. First, Samantha and/or some of her relatives travel into the past. The eight episodes that begin the seventh season, in which Sam and Darrin travel to Salem, at times during the twentieth century and at others back in the seventeenth, form the most important cycle of episodes in which the potential of backward time travel is explored. The show's engagement with the historical reality of Salem is made all the more real by the location shooting used in creating the episodes. *TV Guide* did a cover story on the opening of the seventh season of *Bewitched* because the show went on location to shoot in Salem, a very unusual occurrence for a cheaply produced telefilm sitcom. *Gilligan's Island,* for example, relied on a Los Angeles island set for all one hundred of its episodes, and dream sequences on that show were filmed using barely disguised (with smoke machines) soundstages.

This cycle of *Bewitched* episodes begins with the two-part season opener, "To Go or Not to Go, That Is the Question" and "Salem, Here We Come." These episodes involve surveillance of the Stephenses' marriage by the witches' council, a surveillance that ends in the grudging acceptance of Samantha's love for Darrin when Hepzibah, Queen of the Witches, falls in love with a mortal herself and realizes, in a nutshell, that mortals are people, too. The next two episodes consist of another two-part narrative, "The Salem Saga" (#203, 10/8/70) and "Samantha's Hot Bed Warmer" (#204, 10/15/70), in which an enchanted bed warmer follows Samantha and Darrin out of the House of the Seven Gables. The artifact turns out to be a warlock whom Serena transformed during the witch trials. Seeing Samantha, he assumes she is his tormentor. Sam then has to summon Serena to fix the mess she has inadvertently caused: Darrin has been thrown in jail for stealing the priceless artifact. Sam sends Serena back in time to Puritan Salem to remember the spell. Serena then returns to the present, changes the warlock back, and (since the bed-warmer evidence has disappeared) allows Darrin to escape a jail sentence.

The idea that Serena could have turned a man into a bed warmer during the Salem witch trials and then completely forgotten about it for over three hundred years is remarkable. Given the gender reversal it implies, Serena's power is best compared to a film such as *Vertigo* (Alfred Hitchcock, 1958), also about the power history has on the present. In his reading of the film, Robert Corber states that *Vertigo* fixates on a "counter-history of the United States" (155) that emphasizes how Hispanics such as the discarded Carlotta were denied representation in the American West. Her Anglo lover could get away with such a thing because "men could do such things in those days," the nineteenth century, declares the Argosy bookshop owner, Pops Liebl, in the film. Every bit as concerned with the significance of history on the present, *Bewitched* offers a gender reversal of this Hitchcock masterpiece. Whereas the film demonstrates the replication of the Anglo lover's discarding of Carlotta through its plot about Gavin Elster's use and abandonment of Judy for his scheme to murder his wife, *Bewitched* details Serena's ability to discard the warlock in the midst of the Salem witch trials. While this is, of course, pure fantasy—the witch trials are about male punishment of femininity—other episodes of the Salem storyline are more complicated about the gender significance of witch burning and its history.

The final episode, "Samantha's Old Salem Trip" (#208, 11/12/70), is the best example of this. Esmeralda accidentally zaps Samantha back to Salem during the witch trials, and issues of gender and history become intertwined. One of the crucial pieces of information regarding the gender politics of the show resides in this episode, which grapples directly with the patriarchal persecution of witches in puritanical Salem. In this progressive gender representation, Samantha argues for the rights of women to a fair trial before the town fathers of Salem.

Taken in chains before a tribunal of Puritans, Darrin and Samantha are about to be executed as witches. At the tribunal, she uses her powers to electrify her body, causing the guards to unhand her. After she twitches her nose to break the bonds that bind their hands, Samantha demonstrates that the women the Puritans have been accusing of being witches are guiltless of any wrongdoing. Sam delivers a passionate speech

Sam defends herself from the Puritans, in "Samantha's Old Salem Trip" (11/12/70).

on social justice, ending with the words, "Now, do you understand? The people that you persecuted were guiltless, they were mortals, just like yourselves. You are the guilty."

On the basis of the force of Samantha's magical and rhetorical powers of persuasion, the Puritan judge explains away Samantha's trickery as hallucination, the result of their "witch hysteria," and declares an end to "these and future trials." *Bewitched* performs the work of rescuing the progressive gender implications of witchery and its detractors on the heels of Arthur Miller's *The Crucible,* a 1953 theatrical allegory critical of McCarthyism, and years ahead of academic Mary Daly's radical feminist work on witchery as an emblem of resistance to patriarchy in *Gyn/Ecology.* While *Bewitched* is by no means an allegory in Miller's sense, nor is it radically feminist in Daly's, that it engages in representational practices that resonate with these high cultural and academic artifacts speaks to a need to rescue it from its relegation to the 1960s "vast wasteland."

The other episodes in the Salem storyline cannot be reduced to any given formula as to the gendered meaning of the past. One episode, "Darrin on a Pedestal" (#205, 10/22/70), is particularly interesting because it features both stereotypes of masculinity and a tour-de-force moment of brilliance to save an account by Samantha. In the episode, Serena switches Darrin with the famous sailor at the wheel on the Fisherman's Memorial, enabling the fisherman to lustfully cavort with Serena. Here, Serena's experience confirms the memorial's intent, to celebrate the rugged masculinity of seamen. By the end of the episode, Serena's antics have wreaked their expected havoc with Darrin's business life. With Darrin frozen as a statue, Serena brings the fisherman to the business lunch Larry has set up with client Mr. Barrows regarding an umbrella ad campaign. There, the hard-drinking and loud-singing sailor offends the conservative Barrows, who threatens to take his account to a different agency. However, Samantha arrives and privately convinces Serena to release Darrin from his confinement. As the sailor leaves and Darrin arrives, Samantha implores Mr. Barrows to listen to her explanation. In an embarrassing moment of gentlemanly patriarchy, Mr. Barrows declares: "Mrs. Stephens, I am a businessman most of the time, but I am a gentleman all of the time."

The gender politics of the episode cannot be reduced to this conservative endorsement of gentlemanly tolerance for female kookiness. Instead, Samantha performs another one of her famous salvage operations on Darrin's career. This episode is particularly interesting because, although released from the pedestal, Darrin remains essentially a statue. While Darrin sits stupefied, this time by confusion and not witchcraft, Samantha invents, using her wit and not her magic, an advertising campaign using the "masculine image" of the Fisher-

Sam confronts rugged masculinity, in "Darrin on a Pedestal" (10/22/70).

man's Memorial to sell umbrellas. Mr. Barrows loves Sam's idea, and signs the account with McMann and Tate, without Darrin ever uttering a word. The imagery of the sequence reiterates the important role Samantha has played in the creation of this celebration of masculinity via advertising: rather than Larry's typical punch in the bicep to playfully cap their landing of the account, Larry punches Sam in the arm, who in turn relays the punch to Darrin.

Beyond the Salem episodes, *Bewitched* frequently uses the time-travel plot formation toward other ends. For example, in "The Return of Darrin the Bold" (#217, 2/4/71), Samantha travels back in time to confront one of Darrin's ancestors, a fourteenth-century Irish nobleman. In this episode Dick Sargent plays Darrin. However, Darrin the Bold makes his first appearance four seasons earlier on the show, in episode #79 ("A Most Unusual Wood Nymph," 10/13/66). In that particular episode, Dick York plays Darrin. Through both its time-travel component (Darrin as both domesticated contemporary husband and boorish medieval lord), and its status as a remake (Dick York and Dick Sargent play both Darrin and Darrin the Bold differently), the show is able to grapple with how, why, and to what extent patriarchal relationships have changed. While Samantha remains the same, we get four very different versions of Darrin; his medieval incarnation, Darrin the Bold, is a lecherous, womanizing beast, very different from the controlling, passive-aggressive Darrin of the present. And, as noted earlier, Sargent's Darrin is much edgier than York's genial but exasperated version.

The Darrin the Bold episodes and others of its kind—such as the season 8 opener, "How Not to Lose Your Head to King Henry VIII" (#229 and 230, 9/15/71 and 9/22/71)—structure themselves around the differences historical context makes in the experience of patriarchy by an unchanged Samantha. On the business trip across the European continent that harkens back to Ricky and Lucy Ricardo's famous vacation a decade before, Darrin and Samantha visit the Tower of London. There, Sam frees a nobleman trapped by an evil witch in a painting. The witch retaliates by sending Sam back to the court of King Henry VIII. Having lost her memory—a consequence of time-travel in *Bewitched*'s operating rules—Sam joins a group of traveling bards. As the second part of the episode begins, Endora has sent Darrin back in history to rescue Sam. He must kiss Sam so she will recover her memory and bring them both back to the present.

The specific invocation of Henry VIII in the episode's title refers to his status as a wife murderer. The popular televisual understanding of this is perhaps best illustrated by the appearance of this little slice of British history on the rigged 1950s game show *Twenty One* (NBC, 12/5/56). On this now infamous quiz show, Charles Van Doren and Herb Stempel both successfully recite all of Henry VIII's wives as well as their sometimes-bloody fates. Thus, when the witch sends Sam back to Henry VIII, she is sending her back to be beheaded. Darrin's voyage into the past is at once a heroic quest to save his wife from such a fate, and yet another of the show's allegorical engagements with potential adultery. For when Sam arrives, her beauty, not her powers, bewitch the king, who decides upon her as his next wife. With no memory of Darrin, Sam will do exactly as the king says until Darrin can manage to restore her memory.

The show here contains men's power over women (which is safely located in the past, in the guise of the nuptial beheader), reinforcing the present-day belief in marriage as a mutual contract based on love, which is deemed superior to medieval marriage rituals. Yet the threat to that present-day stability is disturbingly reiterated: with little provocation, Sam can again be in a situation in which she does not remember her husband and instead chooses to marry another man, if not Henry VIII, then some other more appealing figure, such as Rhett Butler from *Gone With the Wind* (Victor Fleming, 1939), as happens in the episode "Samantha Goes South for a Spell."

From Past to Present: George Washington Was a Hippie!

Bewitched employs another strategy to more directly analyze the importance of history: the accidental summoning of a historical figure from the past by one of Samantha's relatives. Although *Bewitched* critics often invoke a "textual decay" model in analyzing the series, claiming *Bewitched* became less and less interesting because the screenwriters simply ran out of ideas, the fifth- and sixth-to-last episodes of the series (#249–50, "George Washington Zapped Here," 2/19/72 and

2/26/72) grapple usefully with the meaning of history. David Marc similarly defends *Bewitched*'s late-run episodes, arguing that: "In sit-coms such as *The Beverly Hillbillies* and *Bewitched,* shows that had elements of the absurd built right into their structure, periods of decay late in their production runs often provided particularly fecund episodes; an unlikely realism gave way to a kind of seedy, primitivistic surrealism, which in turn mingled freely with science fiction" (185).

In the two-part episode about George Washington, the show performs some of its most interesting work on the importance of history. In the episodes, the Stephenses' maid, Esmeralda, accidentally summons the first president into the twentieth century. Going for a walk, he meets hippies and other youthful protestors at the town park. Here, they update Washington on the important events of recent U.S. history. Disturbed by tales of the Vietnam War and police brutality, Washington begins an oration that draws together an ever-enlarging crowd: "Earlier, I stood here and listened to some of you explain what is going on in this country. Things like assassinations, pollution, wars to end wars that do not end wars. This does not please me." A hippie encourages him: "You tell 'em, George." Washington continues: "Where is the voice of the people? Remember what my friend Tom Jefferson said: 'What country can preserve its liberties unless its rulers are warned from time to time that the people preserve the spirit of resistance?'" At this point, a police officer comes to break up Washington's "political rally," since he has no demonstration permit. Bewitched, bothered, and bewildered, Washington declares that the only permit he needs is the Constitution of the United States, and is summarily hauled off to jail when he insists on "running this tyrant through" with his sword.

In an admittedly simplistic yet effective way, this episode reveals some of the large contradictions of an early 1970s culture that purports to be defending American freedoms abroad while at the same time demolishing them at home. The episode performs the same sort of work that a radical historian would do, and resonates with such work being done at that time. Compare, for example, the opening of Howard Zinn's *Post-War America,* a radical history of America from 1945 to 1971, first published in 1971. Zinn opens the book by comparing three historical sites: the eighteenth-century events at Bunker Hill, the 1945 "celebration" of the bombing of Hiroshima, and the 1971 Bunker Hill antiwar protests. Zinn juxtaposes the three events in order to shed critical light on their comparative significance. In the George Washington episode of *Bewitched,* the show engages in a similar historical juxtaposition, asking the crucial question: What might the Founding Fathers think about the protests against the Vietnam War?

Critically, the "George Washington Zapped Here" episodes cannot be said to be characteristic of some general, monolithic politics of *Bewitched.* These episodes are remakes of an earlier two-part episode in which Aunt Clara accidentally summons up Benjamin Franklin into the present: "My Friend Ben" (#87, 12/8/66) and "Samantha for the Defense" (#88, 12/15/66). The "Founding Fathers" scripts, written by two different writers, suggest opposite political stances. Whereas Michael Morris's 1972 script features George Washington's warm engagement with the hippies at the park, James Henerson's 1966 script has Benjamin Franklin berate a hippie in front of the public library for his irreverent dress and surly attitude. As Franklin stands in front of the building, a businessman asks Ben what his costume is attempting to advertise. Franklin replies that he is not advertising anything, he is merely waiting for the library to open. The rude teen hippie insists: "Ah, c'mon, buddy boy. Whadaya pitchin', some movie or somethin'?" Ben berates the youth:

Benjamin Franklin berates a hippie, in "My Friend Ben" (12/8/66).

Young man, in the sense that one may learn a good deal
about a man by his clothing, I am in fact advertising myself, in the same sense that you, by your appearance, pro-
claim what you are. By your clothes and countenance, I
take you to be advertising dirt, slovenliness, and a dislike
for soap and water. Your demeanor proclaims your inso-
lence and your disrespect. And by your speech, I suspect
that you are advertising rudeness, vulgarity, and an igno-
rance of the English language. Good day, sir.

Unlike the "hippie" Washington, who must be dragged to
jail, Franklin himself enforces the moral order.

Whatever the explanation for this profound difference—the differing political sensibilities of Henerson and
Morris, a palpable shift in public response to hippies between 1966 and 1972—the intertextual comparison between
the two episodes makes it clear that the politics of *Bewitched,*

even considering something as basic as its use of history, is fundamentally conflicted, and cannot be reduced to one simple formula. Furthermore, as cultural historical documents, the Founding Fathers episodes of *Bewitched* are by no means anomalous as examples of the "Television Renaissance" or so-called Age of Relevance, a critical gesture that severs *Bewitched* from its historical associations with "the vast wasteland" of the 1960s.

For example, a 1968 episode of *The Smothers Brothers Comedy Hour* performs similar historical analysis. In an episode of that show featuring, of all people, guest star Agnes Moorehead—cinematically famous as Charles Foster Kane's mother, but televisually as Samantha's—there is a skit in which Moorehead again plays a mother, this time of George Washington. As the skit begins, Mrs. Washington is frantically worried about her son, who is again out all night working on "that pointless Declaration of Independence." When George (played by Tommy Smothers) finally does return home, he is accompanied by two redcoats who demand that Mrs. Washington "keep this hippie off of the streets, or we'll have to lock him up for good." Both *The Smothers Brothers Comedy Hour* and *Bewitched* associate George Washington, the "greatest" of the Founding Fathers, not with the U.S. power structure, but with the counterculture hippie movement.

After the police leave, Mrs. Washington berates his protests, grabbing his sign, "Down with King George." Next, Mrs. Washington announces that George has been drafted. George attempts to run away to foment revolution with his friends, but Benedict Arnold knocks on the door. Mrs. Washington tells George to be more like him: "Benedict Arnold, now there's a good boy for you." When Arnold insists, "I'd rather be a redcoat than a dead coat," Agnes Moorehead stops the scene. With the camera zooming in on her, she states, in parody of the Barry Goldwater ad campaign (would

Darrin have devised the "Better dead than Red" campaign?): "In your heart, you know he's right." Washington closes the skit announcing his vision for the new United States, also in close-up:

> It's gonna be a great country. One nation, invisible, with liberty and justice, for most of us. Where all men are created equal, regardless of race, creed, or color. Race and creed, but I don't know about color. . . . This is a country of the people, by the people, instead of the people . . . And Mom, in my honor, they will put my picture on every dollar bill as a symbol that in this country, a buck comes first.

The skit thus takes a similar juxtapositional strategy as *Bewitched* and defends the otherwise televisually scorned antiwar protesters by revealing their historical forebears as no less than the Founding Fathers.

Steven Alan Carr alleges that angry viewers and network executives frequently berated the Smothers Brothers for ridiculing prominent Americans, both past and present (3). That *The Smothers Brothers Comedy Hour* met with wide protest—while *Bewitched* did not, save for a conservative religious critique of the show's endorsement of witchery, familiar in our age with similar protests against Harry Potter— should not be surprising. The political negotiations of *Bewitched* lie buried in a show otherwise assumed to be prime evidence for Newton Minnow's "vast wasteland" of 1960s telefilm situation comedy; yet, given the complex cultural negotiations of the *Bewitched* textual system, it becomes clear that the wasteland hypothesis does a disservice to the richness of *Bewitched* as a cultural artifact.

Bewitched is by no means atypical of 1960s sitcoms in its tendency to represent the significance of history in this way. Almost all good 1960s telefilm sitcoms—*The Beverly Hillbillies, I Dream of Jeannie, The Andy Griffith Show*—employed plots of this sort. A man claiming to be Wyatt Earp came to Mayberry in *The Andy Griffith Show.* Jeannie blinked up Napoleon on *I Dream of Jeannie,* thus exposing the links between the space race spearheaded by Major Nelson and its militarist impetus. Whereas these episodes were anomalous in these other series, they were systemic to *Bewitched*'s representational system, which conjured up historical characters in thirteen different episodes, including Sigmund Freud (episode #84), Queen Victoria (#100), Julius Caesar (#173), and Bonano Pisano (the designer of the leaning tower of Pisa, in episode #232).

Many *Bewitched* episodes explore the politics of history in different ways. Not just reliant on magic, some of the episodes use old-fashioned melodrama to effect this engagement. In "And Then I Wrote" (#45, 11/11/65), Samantha helps an elderly man commemorate the end of the Civil War—the centenary celebration of which occurred the year this episode was in production—by writing the script for a public service campaign engineered by Darrin. Endora helps Sam with her lifeless writing: the witches gain inspiration by zapping the Civil War personages to life to gain historical perspective on the fullness of their characters. In other episodes, such as "We're in for a Bad Spell" (#39, 9/30/65), the injustices of the past are shown to be very much pertinent to the present. In this episode, Darrin has to engage in all sorts of ridiculous behavior (having his friend kiss a dog and dunking him into a swimming pool) in order to remove a curse put upon him by a witch because his ancestor was a judge in Salem. In *Bewitched,* because of the lasting historical power of the witches, the repressed past can resurface at any time and wreak havoc in the present. Here, *Bewitched* is not so far from William Faulkner's famous modernist dictum: "The past is never dead. It's not even past."

A great number of episodes also engage in the comic representation of a number of pressing 1960s and 1970s social issues. As with many other of what Lynn Spigel dubs the "fantastic family sit-coms," such as *I Dream of Jeannie*, *Bewitched* used the hippie critique of what Endora, in "If They Never Met" (#127, 1/25/68), dubs Darrin's "miserable bourgeois existence." Here, Darrin, before meeting Samantha, admits he does not want to marry girlfriend Sheila Sommers because he does not really love her, even though she is beautiful and rich. In the following episode, "Hippie, Hippie, Hooray" (#128, 2/1/68), Samantha's cousin Serena, who embraces a swinging single lifestyle (and dresses the hippie part), is used as a counterpoint to Sam's embrace of traditional family values.

Bewitched's deep ambivalence toward such traditional roles is one of its constitutive features. In the episode that was broadcast two weeks prior, "Snob in the Grass" (#126, 1/11/68), Sheila, Darrin's ex-girlfriend and the daughter of a current client, insults Sam's boring, married lifestyle. As she did in the show's pilot, which also featured Sheila attempting to embarrass Sam, Sam eventually uses her magic to expose the woman to public ridicule. Here, the show is at its most conservative, and Sam's magic is not a liberational force for women, but instead a tool for the maintenance of patriarchal values, endorsing marriage over empowered women's late 1960s single lifestyles. The Serena episodes, which contrast the different lifestyles of Sam and her cousin, end without punishing Sam's hippie doppelgänger (both women are, of course, played by Elizabeth Montgomery). Instead, Serena flies away, unrepentant, for causing Darrin trouble, and, much to Sam's exasperation, continues her hedonistic lifestyle in which she is more interested in having fun than apologizing to Darrin.

Some *Bewitched* episodes use the possibilities of magic to engage otherwise censorable issues concerning sexual politics. "Mixed Doubles" (#221, 3/4/71), for example, allegorizes the possibilities of spouse swapping, foregrounded cinematically a few years earlier in Paul Mazursky's *Bob and*

Carol and Ted and Alice (1969). Because she has been worrying so hard about the health of Larry and Louise Tate's relationship, Sam wakes up one day having willed herself into Louise's body. We see Sam in Larry's bedroom the next morning, even though Larry sees her as Louise. Conversely, Sam knows that Louise is now living with Darrin, even though the other characters, because they are mortal, sense nothing wrong. While Dr. Bombay eventually fixes the inversion, Samantha—as well as we spectators in the audience—knows that for twenty-three minutes, the span of two days in the characters' lives, Darrin and Sam and Larry and Louise lived an alternative, radical marital lifestyle.

Throughout the episode, the imposed sexual normalcy of the mortal world is held in stark contrast to the libertinism of the witches, and particularly the warlocks. When Dr. Bombay first arrives, he is wearing a clown outfit. He makes one of his bad puns, this time of a sexual nature: "Endora caught me clowning around with my nurse." Later, Dr. Bombay hits on Endora, asking her: "Care to come up to my pad for a nightcap?" The asexual Endora pops away in disgust. We know, however, that Dr. Bombay's uncontrolled libido will return in another episode. No matter what the conservative resolution to the mortal plotline—Sam will return to her husband Darrin and Louise to Larry—the alternative world of the witches and warlocks continues on unfettered by traditional morality.

"Oh My Stars!": *Bewitched* and the Space Race

The contemporary issue *Bewitched* engages most directly concerns domestic family life as inflected by the historical conditions of the cold war. As noted earlier, Lynn Spigel studies one set of implications of this, the discursive relationship between the 1960s U.S. space program and the telefilm sitcom, in part by analyzing *I Dream of Jeannie,* about a genie in a bottle working for her "master," American astronaut Tony Nelson. While discussing Jeannie's power to zap herself into Major Nelson's space capsule at the mere folding of her arms and nodding of her head, Spigel states the following in a footnote: "A similar situation occurred in a 1967 episode of *Bewitched* when Samantha claims that she has beaten the astronauts to the moon through her magical powers of transportation" (234). In invoking this moment as a site that engages the history of the U.S. space program, Spigel provides a useful jumping-off point for a more in-depth look at *Bewitched's* engagement with the space race.

The episode to which Spigel refers, "Sam in the Moon" (#91, 1/5/67), ridicules the epic 1960s quest to send a man to the moon. In doing so, the teaser to "Sam in the Moon" may be one of the most significant ninety seconds on all of 1960s American television. Pursuant to Spigel's thesis that the 1960s fantastic family sitcom forwards a gender discourse directly at odds with NASA's masculinist conquest of space, the segment establishes Samantha's valuation of feminine domestic labor as superior to the exploration of space.

The episode begins with a long shot of Darrin, sitting on the family living room couch, with their wood-paneled television set in the left foreground of the image. Darrin is leaning forward, in rapt attention. From the male voice-over narrator on the television program, we learn that he is watching special events news coverage of a manned moon probe. The narrator intones: "This picture was taken two months ago by a camera aboard an unmanned space capsule." In the middle of the voice-over, the editor cuts to a close-up of the television set, whose image in turn is comprised of a close-up of the moon, a real photographic image taken by NASA. Suddenly, an unidentified humming noise on the soundtrack accompanies the image of the moon deteriorating into snowy static on the television. The editor cuts to a medium shot of Darrin, who turns to his right and says to Samantha, off-screen left: "Sam, not now, I'm watching the moon probe." Next, a long shot of Sam running the vacuum cleaner reveals that Sam does not understand. Darrin explains, "When you turn on the vacuum cleaner, the set goes flooey." Female domestic labor has suddenly impinged upon boyish Darrin's delight in the exploits of the male NASA astronauts.

Darrin shouts, "I can't see," but since immediately before, Sam has turned off the appliance, he appears ridiculous shouting in the now quiet house. As he approaches the television with a gleeful look on his face, Sam walks behind him, explaining, "Sweetheart, I've been waiting for weeks to give the house a thorough cleaning. These rugs are filthy." Initially, Darrin cannot fathom the reasons why his wife's disinterest is so different from his innocent delight: "How can you worry about the dirt on the rugs when we are about to see the surface of the moon?" We cut to a two-shot, over Darrin's shoulder at Samantha, as she jokes: "The moon could use a vacuuming too. All that dust. Yuck."

Samantha's reiteration of her domestic position is put into direct competition with the male commentator, who simultaneously spouts technical evaluations of the mission: "We have now received word from the Cape that the orbit and attitude of the capsule are perfect. In a matter of hours, astronauts aboard the spacecraft will have the closest view of the moon ever seen by the naked eye, thus bringing nearer the day when men will actually land on the moon." Because Samantha is a witch, whose relatives are continuously zapping themselves into outer space—in the episode "What Makes Darrin Run" (#191, 2/12/70), Endora returns from Venus in a NASA space suit—what lurks behind this sequence is the competition that Samantha's female powers pose for NASA's masculinist assumptions. While the television commentator and Darrin believe this mission will produce the closest view ever of the surface of the moon, Samantha knows—as do we, since we watch *Bewitched* every week—that this is patently naïve and untrue.

Now aligned perfectly with the television commentator, Darrin implores Sam to watch the event with him, stressing its importance in first their relationship and then in the history of a very specifically American civilization: "Honey, why don't you forget about the housework for a while? Watch this with me. Pretty interesting, even for a sophisticated witch like you." Darrin at first jokes with Samantha about her witchery, believing that NASA's technical wizardry is one of the few things that could possibly compete with her "natural" powers. After giving her a kiss does not work to convince her, he invokes the full weight of American history to establish the gravity, if you will, of the situation: "It's like having a ringside seat for the discovery of America. Aren't you interested?"

At this point, the deliberately transnational Samantha—she and her mother are as comfortable in Japan or Paris as they are in the Connecticut suburbs of New York City—unleashes her logic, for which Darrin's boyish delight in the space program has no answer. Sam deflects the masculinist mastery of space through which the television commentator speaks, demonstrating knowledge far superior to his own, and certainly to Darrin's: "Well, certainly I'm interested. But it's the same elliptical orbit, isn't it? Oh, I mean except that this time the pilots will see for themselves the mile-high dust drifts and the lunar craters." Samantha's knowledge of technology motif runs throughout the show. In a remarkable teaser segment to the early episode, "Just One Happy Family" (#10, 11/19/64), an unethical television repairman takes apart Sam's set so that he may charge her for a whole day's repair work. When she catches wind of the man's scheme, Sam twitches the set back together while he has his back turned, to the repairman's shock.

In the "Sam in the Moon" episode as well, Samantha dismisses the technical knowledge of the space program, re-asserting her principal interest in the domestic labor to which she has committed herself: "I am more interested in getting the refrigerator straightened out, the oven scrubbed, the attic cleaned, and the rugs vacuumed." This is certainly prime evidence for the conservative nature of *Bewitched*: Samantha prefers homemaking to any other pursuit the universe has to offer. However, in this context, her gender politics are too complicated to make such a reductive claim. Samantha here calls Darrin on his patriarchal bluff: Within their relationship, he has insisted that Sam put the care of his household above all of her other interests. When she does so, and it interferes with his pleasure, he suddenly changes the rules. To label Samantha's behavior as purely subservient to patriarchy when she refuses to submit to Darrin's whims does not seem to do justice to their more nuanced relationship.

This insistence on living the life that Darrin has assigned her marks Samantha's behavior in "Sam in the Moon" as distinct from other episodes of *Bewitched*. For example, at the end of the pilot, Darrin and Sam return late at night from a dinner party to a kitchen full of dirty dishes. When Darrin kisses her amorously and insists she come to bed for love-making instead of doing the dishes, she at first refuses. He implores further that she can do them tomorrow night. Samantha observes, "That's what you said last night." When Darrin submits and tells her to hurry while he awaits her in bed (it does not occur to him to help her clean), Samantha looks at the huge pile of work, and zaps the kitchen clean. In an ironic gesture that predicts Samantha's perpetual inability to abide by Darrin's prohibition against witchcraft in the forthcoming 253 episodes, Samantha jokes, "Well, maybe I can taper off."

By the time of "Sam in the Moon," ninety episodes later, Samantha is demonstrating what this "tapering off" looks like. The episode begins where the pilot's ending left off: Samantha now insists that she will not succumb to Darrin's distractions from the chores. Rather than watching the moon probe, Samantha toils at the work Darrin forces her to do, yet which she insists she does willingly.

"Sam in the Moon" does not dwell on this patriarchal contradiction. Instead, the teaser immediately moves toward a different crisis that will drive the episode. "Anyway, I've seen the moon," Samantha declares as she walks out of the room, on her way to continue the housework. In reaction to this, the camera dollies into a medium close-up of Darrin's face, as he echoes, "She's seen the moon." The worried expression on his face causes us to realize that it has now dawned on him that this might mean Sam has in fact been to the moon. The credits roll—an animated sequence in which Samantha flies into her kitchen on a broom, a feat NASA only wishes it could accomplish—at this moment of crisis for the patriarchal imagination.

The rest of the episode features Darrin grappling with the consequences of the teaser. In his hysteria over her declaration, Darrin believes that Samantha has brought moon dust into the house from a trip to the moon, so he takes it to a local pharmacist for analysis. In a fit of panic, he then realizes that he may have inadvertently "outed" Samantha as a witch. Luckily for Darrin, and in a nice bit of writing that only reinforces the character of Sam's total dedication to all things domestic, the mystery substance turns out to be the fruit of Sam's household labor, the dust from the vacuum cleaner. While this particular episode merely indicts Darrin's paranoia, other episodes reveal that Sam travels the cosmos with an effortless twitch of her nose all the time. For example, she joins Serena at the "Cosmos Cotillion" on some unnamed planet far out in space in the episode "Serena Stops the Show" (#192, 2/19/70).

Despite its detailed evidence for Spigel's excellent study

Darrin tries to protect Sam's secret from NASA, in "Sam in the Moon" (1/5/67).

of the televisual gendering of the 1960s U.S. space program, the more important legacy of "Sam in the Moon" is that it brings into focus one of the overarching thematic concerns of the show: family life in the age of cold war surveillance. While Darrin worries over whether he has exposed Sam's secret, he has a waking nightmare in which NASA scientists prod and probe her for secrets in their desperate attempt to beat the Russians to the moon. As with other more serious 1960s shows obsessed with surveillance and control, such as the anti-McCarthyite *The Fugitive* (ABC, 1963–67), *Bewitched* critiques the legacy of the cold war surveillance state, again contrasting the show quite favorably to Robert Corber's reading of Alfred Hitchcock masterpieces such as *Rear Window* (1954), a defense of a man who spies on his neighbor.

As noted earlier, the opening two seasons of *Bewitched* are, in fact, built around this concern, expressed in the guise of the busybody neighbor Gladys Kravitz. Later seasons back away from this surveillance focus and turn toward other issues studied in this book. As one statistical piece of evidence for this claim, out of seventy-four episodes shown during the first two seasons, twenty-eight feature Alice Pearce in the role of Gladys Kravitz. In the remaining five seasons, comprising over twice as many (180) episodes, Sandra Gould, the actress who replaced Pearce in the role of Gladys, appears only twenty-nine times. In the early black-and-white episodes, Kravitz's incessant surveillance of the Stephenses' household results in countless close calls for the revelation of Sam's secret. This thread of the show's interest is begun in the second episode, "Be It Ever So Mortgaged," in which Gladys watches in shock as Endora and Samantha zap different landscapes around the new house on 1164 Morning Glory Circle, as discussed previously.

The episode "I Confess" (#135, 4/4/68) most fully thematizes the stakes of *Bewitched*'s critique of the cold war surveillance state. As such, I will use a detailed discussion of it to cap my analysis of *Bewitched* as a show that historicizes its own present. The episode begins with Darrin refusing to let Sam use witchcraft to get the gloves she has forgotten in the restaurant where they have just finished dinner. Darrin goes back inside to get them himself, in the "normal" mortal way. In the meantime, the town drunk (played as always by Dick Wilson) accosts Sam on the street while she is waiting for Darrin to return. While usually a comic figure who merely has another drink when he sees Samantha pop into the room unannounced, the drunk is more aggressive in this episode, demanding that Samantha come home with him. When Samantha uses magic to douse him with a bucket of water, Darrin objects, not to the drunk's behavior, but to Sam's.

In their bedroom that night, Sam and Darrin fight over their respective behaviors. Fed up with issuing prohibitions against witchcraft, Darrin gives up. "Let's stop being hyp-

ocrites. Let's tell the whole world your true identity," he says
in a huff. Knowing what a bad idea this is, Sam casts a spell
over Darrin to make him dream what life would be if the
whole world knew their secret. In the first scene of the
dream, Darrin tells Larry the truth about Sam. "Samantha is
different," says Darrin. "I'm a witch," says Sam. She is forced
to do some magic to convince him when he thinks they are
having a joke at his expense. Once convinced, Larry immediately gets the idea "to control the world." Larry wants to
"juggle the stock market and seize control of the national
economy." He enthuses in a megalomaniac tone: "I've wanted
to rule the world ever since I was a little kid." When Darrin
and Samantha refuse to help Larry with his plan for world
domination, Larry fires Darrin yet again.

In another dream, set a few weeks later, the whole
world knows the secret. Abner Kravitz is selling seats on his
lawn for the witch watchers. On his way home, Darrin is
mobbed for autographs by a crowd of fanatics. Darrin rushes
into the house with his suit torn to pieces. The phone rings
incessantly. One phone call is from Mickey Mantle, asking
for Sam's help playing baseball. He wants to bat .600. Sam refuses to help him, declaring, "I'm a Mets fan." They have to
change their phone number ten times. Darrin cannot get a
job. Tabitha is depressed because none of her friends will
play with her because Sam refuses to zap up ponies for them
to ride on. Darrin laments: "Poor kid, why should she be
punished for my mistake?" The climax of the nightmare occurs when Brigadier General Stanton and "Agent W" from
the CIA come to visit. They insist, for national security reasons, that the family be moved into protective custody. "A
nice concentration camp atmosphere," Darrin laments. Sam
zaps them into the desert, where they now must live in a
trailer, behind a chain link fence, guarded by MPs. At "inter-
rogation time," a jeep takes Sam and Tabitha away from Darrin, who is left behind the fence standing on the desolate

The Stephens family is jailed in a concentration camp, in "I Confess" (4/4/68).

concrete. Darrin screams, "Let me out!" as he wakes up from his dream.

At breakfast the next morning, Sam playfully tells Darrin that she now agrees with him, that she wants to tell the world their secret. "I want to breathe the air of truthfulness," she enthuses. Darrin refuses in a panic, having been taught his lesson about keeping things the way they are. This episode offers a caustic critique of the national security state. In a culture in which being a good American is so rigidly defended, the episode goes to great lengths to expose such behavior as devastatingly destructive. In no clearer way could *Bewitched* cut against the grain of American ideology: the exposure of difference is not tolerated in American culture in this nightmare vision. Such exposure leads quite clearly to concentration camps and military arrest.

For the reasons I have outlined throughout this book, *Bewitched* cannot be reduced to a single formula with a stable political cant. The show offers contradictory political engagements with the meaning of history depending on context. The Salem episodes use voyages into the past to variously argue for feminist liberation and the preservation of traditional masculinity. Episodes featuring the Founding Fathers represent the colonial Americans as proto-hippies but also as cultural conservatives. Such contradictory stances are also found in storylines that represent contemporary American culture, with episodes sometimes flirting with the endorsement of alternative lifestyles, and sometimes desperately arguing for the preservation of traditional family life.

A Metatextual Masterpiece

124

In some of its most fascinating episodes, *Bewitched* dealt with the history—the back stories—of its own characters. This became tricky because the show was forced to replace Dick York after the fifth season due to his increasing back problems. While the casting change of a main character could not possibly go unnoticed, the show takes a particularly modernist stance in how it deals with the radical physical transformation of Darrin Stephens in the summer of 1969.

As noted earlier, the "textual decay" model (suggesting that innovative early episodes of long-running shows eventually give way to hackneyed plots as the writers run out of new plot ideas) is one of the commonplaces of *Bewitched* criticism. Gerald Jones unambiguously forwards this theory of decline: "*Bewitched* was a savvy show when it started, simply by virtue of its acknowledgment of female power. Just a few years later shifting trends had rendered it merely quaint. As if in a trade-off, it flirted with liberal politics in the late '60s, turning out a few bland sermons about race prejudice. The changing scene was too much for it, however; its ratings plummeted in 1969" (180).

David Marc's theory of *Bewitched*'s textual devolution is more nuanced. Marc's model contends that the show moved through three stages during its eight-year run: "introduction, maturation, and decay." He characterizes the introduction phase episodes as "limited to a circumspect domestic world shared by intimate personae—one natural, the other super-natural" (134). He then suggests that the show matured to deal with more complex relationships between the mortal and supernatural characters, followed by an increasing de-cline: "As with *My Favorite Martian,* the writers seemed to go crazy looking for variations with the passing of the seasons" (140). Marc links what I consider the show's most interesting interventions to its decay as "th[e] cautious balance between sit-com realism and sit-com fantasy collapsed. Time-travel was instituted, including a visit to the court of Henry VIII" (134).

Where Marc sees time travel as a bellwether of narrative decay, I find the time-travel episodes to be some of the most culturally significant exemplars of the show. Because they universally pan the later episodes, these "decay" analyses miss some significant work done when later episodes revisit or remake earlier episodes. Rather than characterizing such remakes as tired retreads of already-used plotlines, I suggest that these episodes use an innovative, modernist tack to grapple with a potentially disastrous production problem: the need to replace Dick York.

The decision to replace the original actor with Dick Sargent remains, to this day, one of the show's primary means of camp identification. In the comedy film *Wayne's World* (Penelope Spheeris, 1992), local-access cable TV show host Wayne makes fun of the stupidity of *Bewitched*'s producers when he explains: "Dick York, Dick Sargent. Didn't they think we'd notice? Duh." In the mid-1990s, Nick at Nite used their usual camp strategy to call attention to the shift—which they assume the show attempts to keep hidden—with a viewer poll as to who viewers like best: Dick York, "Nick at Nite's [black and white] Darrin," or the "other guy" only available in color reruns on other cable stations.[9]

Dick York himself expressed concern over the textual handling of his departure. His proposed solution neatly summarizes what a "realist" approach should have done: "[T]hey should have changed the character completely. . . . Darrin should have been killed off or he and Samantha should have gotten a divorce" (qtd. in Pilato 49). However, Dick York's belief in realism is not exactly in keeping with the narrative logic of the show. Instead, the producers developed a fantastical solution to the problem that has never been adequately appreciated. I believe the handling of the replacement of York by Sargent stands as *Bewitched*'s crowning narrative achievement, and is the closest the show ever gets to the modernist standards by which most contemporary textual study measures aesthetic brilliance.

The camp detractors of the handling are right in that the show makes no gesture in the dialogue to address the replacement. Yet instead of a realist solution, *Bewitched* creates a metatextual mode for dealing with the shift and avoids engaging in a plot trajectory that would stretch credibility: Why would Sam and Darrin have gotten a divorce, if they so obviously loved each other in the previous episode? The first episode Dick Sargent filmed, "Samantha's Better Halves" (#185, 1/1/70, that is, New Year's Day!), is a remake of the Dick York second season episode "Divided He Falls" (#69, 5/5/66).

The Sargent episode involves a flashback to the time when Endora split Darrin into two. Yet in the flashbacks, Dick Sargent, not Dick York, plays Darrin. The show handles the transition of York to Sargent by projecting Sargent back into both the past of this one episode and all of the past episodes of *Bewitched*. All of this is perfectly in keeping with the logic of *Bewitched,* in which summoning people from the past and traveling to the past oneself are commonly done. Furthermore, the radical components of replacing Darrin within the diegesis of the show further illuminates the complexity of the later episodes, which critics such as David Marc identify as "decadent," that is, less well done than the "mature" episodes featuring Dick York.

The sudden and unexplained change in Darrin's appearance in fact is a more normal event in *Bewitched*'s universe because of the series' basic premises. For example, Darrin is often being transformed, or threatened to be transformed, into some animal or inanimate object by one of Sam's fiendishly mischievous relatives: an artichoke in "Mother Meets What's His Name" (#4, 10/8/64), a mouse in "Samantha's Secret Spell" (#179, 11/13/69), a donkey in "If the Shoe Pinches" (#197, 3/26/70), a pig in "This Little Piggie" (#220, 2/25/71), and a statue in "Darrin on a Pedestal" (#205, 10/22/70). Even more illuminating is "A Change of Face" (#33, 5/13/65). As discussed earlier, Endora and Samantha play with Darrin while he is sleeping, altering his face so that it better pleases their aesthetic sensibilities. When Darrin awakens and discovers what the witches have done to him, he storms off to his local bar. Feeling terrible about what she has done, Samantha transforms herself into a sexy woman with a French accent. Even though he has forgiven her, Darrin plays along with Sam, pretending not to know it is she, and has the last laugh at her jealous expense. In a world where both Darrin and Sam change appearances in so many episodes, the magical appearance of Dick Sargent's interpretation of Darrin is not so odd as would have been, say, the replacement of Dick Van Dyke's Rob on *The Dick Van Dyke Show*.

Through its reliance on remakes, ultimately, the history *of the show* becomes part and parcel of the history *in the show*, and is dealt with using remarkably similar methods. This elegant narrative solution to a terrible production problem

127

should ensure *Bewitched* a place in academic television criticism other than as a "vast wasteland" telefilm sitcom. Unfortunately, the extensive use of remakes to erase Dick York from the representational universe has not received nearly the attention as the last episode of the MTM quality television show *Newhart* (CBS, 1982–90). In that episode, the Vermont innkeeper, Dick Loudon (Bob Newhart), wakes up at the end of the long-running show in Chicago, not with Joanna (Mary Frann), his Vermont wife, but instead with Emily Hartley (Suzanne Pleshette), his wife from his earlier series, *The Bob Newhart Show* (CBS, 1972–78), in which he played a Chicago psychiatrist.

One piece of evidence that has been offered to support arguments for the Sargent episodes' weakness has always been that many of them were remakes of scripts already filmed by Dick York. While from an institutional perspective these remakes were clearly done due to the demands of harried shooting schedules and perhaps a dearth of new script ideas, from this analytical perspective sensitive to the metatextual nature of Dick Sargent's relationship to Dick York as Darrin, the remake strategy could be seen as part of the systematic erasure of Dick York from the Stephenses' universe.

The *Bewitched* remake episodes also offer some of the show's most progressive moments. For example, "George Washington Zapped Here" (#249, 2/14/72) is a remake of "My Friend Ben" (#87, 12/8/66), in which Aunt Clara mistakenly summons Benjamin Franklin into the Stephens house. As previously discussed, James Henerson's script for this earlier episode uses the encounter between Franklin and a hippie at the park as a way of conservatively berating the counterculture by way of the smug superiority of the Founding Fathers. But Michael Morris's new script alters the original's premise, having George Washington *support* the counterculture's critique of Darrin's bourgeois hypocrisy, pushing as far as the more radical *Smothers Brothers Comedy Hour* skit in which Agnes Moorehead berates George for his hanging around with hippies.

Throughout its run, *Bewitched* builds a narrative universe in which multiple directions for the characters are explored. As one final example, in the episode "What Every Young Man Should Know" (#72, 5/26/66), Endora tries once again to break up Sam's marriage, this time by showing her what would have happened had she told Darrin she was a witch, not on their wedding night, as happens in the pilot, but on an earlier date. As Sam comes out of the past, she screams at Darrin, "Coward!" Just as Endora's plan seems destined to work, Darrin intervenes, demanding that Endora send him into the past so that he can see the whole scene play out. This second time, Darrin comes to his senses and sticks up for Samantha. Despite Endora repeatedly popping Darrin out of the apartment with Samantha, as she did in the pilot, Darrin keeps coming back to his beloved. He finally shouts his marriage proposal to Sam, hopping mad at Endora's interference. Out of the past for a second time, the episode ends happily, with Endora lamenting, "Isn't that sickening," to Darrin and Sam's passionate kissing.

This book began with a call for less reductive approaches to *Bewitched* than previous academic critical work on the show, which has often used the pilot film as indicative of the entire eight-year run of the series. I end with emphasis on the late remake episodes that, if mentioned at all, are seen as indicative of the show's decay. I propose that the gesture of remaking episodes, if one follows the narrative logic of the show carefully, is part of its most radical narrative solution, the historical reconstruction of an entire back story to account for the need to replace one of the show's central characters. In building such an argument, I have pursued Horace Newcomb's idea that interesting shows build narrative cumulatively, making us care about characters through nuanced repetition. That *Bewitched* accomplished the creation of such a complex narrative universe within the depths of the "wasteland" era is an indication that our historiography of American television needs to be rendered more complex.

Conclusion: Television in the Aura of Film

The relationship between film and television has haunted my approach to *Bewitched*. I write as a contemporary film critic who also finds an intense passion for particular television shows. I have argued against the dominance of a filmic model of narrative for the analysis of television. I also argued that it would be impossible to appreciate *Bewitched* without considering its intertextual relationship to classical Hollywood films, such as *Bell, Book and Candle* and *I Married a Witch*. However, something larger is at stake. As a popular culture analyst, I make no distinction between loving *Bewitched* and the cinema. To me, they are the same thing, audio-visual worlds in which meaning is contested.

I conclude this study with a reflection on its contributions to media criticism. I know of no better place to turn than a neglected film studies book that expresses the importance of hermeneutic interpretation for declaring one's opinions about the culture as well as one's love of audio-visual texts. In *Film in the Aura of Art*, Dudley Andrew explores art cinema in intertextual dialogue with high culture. While Andrew's topic could not be further from my focus here, an examination of a low culture telefilm sitcom beloved by generations of American children, the passion with which Andrew argues is indeed congruent with my passion for *Bewitched*. Andrew concludes his book with a startling inspiration: "[W]e shall not hesitate to call interpretation an 'art' and to be satisfied with it as a way, the best way, of participating in history. It is after all just as insubstantial and as important as the art of living" (201).

As I spent year after year coming back to my *Bewitched* notes, watching and rewatching episodes, alone and with my family, I always knew that the show, for all its silliness, was in fact engaged in a meaningful cultural project, about feminism, about history, about the cold war. This book has argued for similar intertextual connections between the audiovisual texts, the 254 episodes of the show that are *Bewitched,* and its cultural contexts (the space race, the Salem witch trials, the hippie movement), a similar pursuit to Andrew's analysis of the relationship between *Henry V* (Laurence Olivier, 1944) and medieval art (131–51).

I do not mean to gloss over the differences in content between this work and Andrew's. Clearly Andrew finds value in a higher range of artifacts than I do. But at the heart of his hermeneutic method is the idea that one should let what is interesting about the text before you lead where it may. The many episodes of *Bewitched* led me to so many places that I had to write about them or find myself incapable of expressing what I saw to be their cultural value. What Andrew means by aura in his book—a Benjaminian redemption—I find in *Bewitched* and its confluence with popular Hollywood cinema. Andrew finds that value elsewhere, higher on the cultural chain of being. But if we are to fully understand our culture, we need to appreciate both interests. While *Bewitched* should not be valorized at the *expense* of *Diary of a Country Priest* (Robert Bresson, 1951) and the films of Kenji Mizoguchi, other Andrew case studies, it should be recognized as culturally valuable in *tandem* with them.

Bewitched can be seen rightly within an aura that is more popular than that of painting, theater, and the traditional arts. I want to reflect on the significance of using such a Benjaminian term as aura to describe television's contact with the cinema via an analysis of the recent Hollywood film version of

Bewitched (Nora Ephron, 2005). For not only was the 1960s *Bewitched* constructed under the aura of Hollywood cinema (its intertextual reworking of *I Married a Witch* and *Bell, Book and Candle*), but it also has become a cultural benchmark through which we understand ourselves at present.

The film version of *Bewitched* exists in the aura of this fundamentally important television show. It cannot be measured separately from that aura, as its critics have assumed. In his relatively positive review of the film, Roger Ebert writes: "I have never seen a single episode of *Bewitched*. . . . That makes me well-prepared to review the new movie, since I have nothing to compare it with and have to take it on its own terms." As a stand-alone film, *Bewitched* is certainly far worse than Ebert suggests in his review; as a kind of filmic equivalent of my book, it is a breathtaking exercise. That is to say, Nora Ephron's *Bewitched* captures, not the spirit of the original show, which many of the show's fans were looking for, but instead an amalgamation of the many things that *Bewitched* was, aesthetically, narratively, and ideologically.

The film concerns a fading actor, Jack Wyatt (Will Ferrell), who is cast as Darrin in a television remake of *Bewitched*. One day in a bookstore, he spots Isabel Bigelow (Nicole Kidman), who is able to replicate Elizabeth Montgomery's nose twitch. The twist is that Isabel is actually a witch who has moved to the San Fernando Valley in order to live the "normal, mortal way." Jack and Isabel fall in love, fight, and then kiss at the end of the film, in classic romantic comedy fashion.

Littered with moments that can only be properly understood through intimacy with the television show, *Bewitched* the film is a sort of critical reflection on the variety of *Bewitched* episodes as I have studied them in this book. For example, during the credit sequence, as Isabel lands in Los Angeles and uses witchcraft to rent a beautiful picket-fenced house, she gleefully uses the garage door opener to reveal a shiny new yellow Volkswagen in the garage. In this one moment, the film constructs itself out of the building blocks of individual *Bewitched* episodes, in this case "Open the Door Witchcraft" and "Driving Is the Only Way to Fly," two episodes studied in detail earlier in this book. Does one need to know these episodes to understand the film? No, of course not, but if one does know these moments, as the film's creators must, and the readers of this book now do, then the film suddenly becomes much more than an embarrassing misfire at capturing the magic of the 1960s television show. In short, Ephron's and Kidman's *Bewitched* now inhabits, securely and fascinatingly, the aura of Asher's and Montgomery's *Bewitched*.

Within moments, we find Isabel at Bed Bath and Beyond, shopping for towels to put in her new home's bathroom. She is beset by her father, Nigel (Michael Caine), an odd combination of the original's Endora (loving but too involved in Samantha's life) and Maurice (although Nigel is much kinder to Isabel than Maurice was to Samantha). The film immediately engages the sexual libertinism of the warlock lifestyle as I have studied it in episodes such as "Mixed Doubles." Nigel thinks it is fantastic that his life is all instant gratification, something from which Isabel is trying to escape. Throughout the film, Nigel keeps popping in to Isabel's life, much as Endora did on the television show, yet each time engaging a different episode of the original show. For example, at one point, while Isabel is grocery shopping, Nigel talks to Samantha from the surface of a Gorton's fish sticks box, recalling the episode about masculinity, "Darrin on a Pedestal," in which Serena switches Darrin with the famous Gloucester fisherman statue.

Bewitched playfully mixes fidelity to the original show (Isabel actually has a bumbling Aunt Clara) with new innovations. The most significant change, given my interest in 1960s telefilm aesthetics and their relationship to the dominance of proscenium shooting, is that the 2005 film is shot with one camera like the original, but the remake television show within the film is being shot proscenium style, before a live studio audience. After seeing both Isabel and Jack watch the actual pilot of the show in their own bedrooms, we see the opening scene—in which Sam and Darrin literally run into each other on the street—being filmed. When Jack falls, using the physical comedy talents of Will Ferrell, the live studio audience howls in appreciation. Then, in a scene not part of the original pilot, Endora reveals herself to Darrin in the honeymoon suite. When Iris Smythson (Shirley MacLaine), the actress playing Endora, emerges out of the smoke on the set, she nods and bows to the audience, a self-reflexive gesture that horrifies the show's producers and director.

The filmmakers then engage in a remarkable contradiction: they accomplish a freeze effect within the proscenium shooting technique. Reacting to the acknowledgment that his wife is a witch and her mother-in-law is in their honeymoon suite, Darrin declares, "I think I need a drink." The director calls out "Freeze" as a stagehand runs out onto the stage to put a smoking drink in Darrin's hand. The proscenium audience is asked to witness the production process behind *Bewitched*'s special effects, something that was hidden by the original one-camera shooting technique.

The film continues its cataloging of *Bewitched* episodes, even amid the shooting of the pilot. In the scene in which Sam uses magic on Sheila, Darrin's ex-girlfriend, who has staged a dinner party to humiliate Samantha, Isabel likewise uses magic on Jack for humiliating her. When the director asks Isabel if she understands the scene, she details her understanding of the film *we* in the audience are watching: "He tricked me because he's a self-centered has-been." Jack has to deliver a line about a dog, a witty reflection on audience testing that indicates that ratings increase when animals and children appear on the screen; there was, of course, no dog in the actual *Bewitched* pilot.

Isabel punishes Jack by casting a spell on his acting and language abilities, forcing him to deliver the line, "It's my dog," in increasingly absurd ways. At first, Jack performs the moment with a Shakespearean flourish—"Where art thou, dog? Thy canine lover. Where is your hot breath upon the nape of my neck. . . . You shall lick my face and I shall lick your snout"—recalling, of course, the original *Bewitched* episode, "Samantha's Good News," in which Maurice engaged in absurdly pompous Shakespearean recitations to prove his love for Endora. This one scene becomes itself a catalog of many original *Bewitched* episodes. The sequence ends with Jack only being able to speak Spanish, a reference to original language problem episodes such as "Business, Italian Style" and "Samantha and Darrin in Mexico City," analyzed earlier.

In his poison pen review of the film—"a showbiz self-suck unrivaled in modern times for smugness, vapidity, and condescension. To spend even ten minutes in the movie's universe is to experience the Sartrean nausea of an utterly hollow head and heart"—*Village Voice* critic Michael Atkinson laments the show's "postmod" pastiche. This would be accurate had not the *Bewitched* film used these wild postmodern references to implicitly define the similarities and differences between 1960s and 2000s American culture.

As all romantic comedies do, the film ends in perfect continuity with the 1960s *Bewitched*. Uncle Arthur (Steve Carell) appears to Jack and convinces him to fight for Isabel's love. Jack does so, catching Isabel on the soundstage, right in front of the replica of the Morning Glory Circle house. Jack begs Isabel not to leave him. Isabel laments, "I can't be normal because I'm a witch." Jack explains that he understands this because he knows Samantha's story, "caught between two worlds, but she lived happily every after." Jack declares his love for Isabel, and they kiss.

An epilogue, six months later as Jack drives up to his new house, wraps up the film. Replicating "Be It Ever So Mortgaged," in which Sam and Endora use magic to conceive of the property with full landscaping, the film's Mrs. Kravitz begins her snooping, witnessing the effects of Isabel's magic as a tree—in fact, the willow tree from "Weep No More My Willow"—visibly grows in the front yard.

The film version of *Bewitched* does not engage the same historical material as did the 1960s television show. It is not obsessed with cold war surveillance: Isabel does magic whenever she pleases—she reverses time with a rewind button (something that Samantha never did), subtly, to have breakfast before 11 a.m., and severely, to change the outcome of her relationship with Jack—without any fear of consequences. And the business context of the original *Bewitched* is completely absent: there is no Larry Tate, and no threat to Jack's well-being if he does not conform to the normative patterns of Darrin's advertising culture. In short, Ephron's *Bewitched* is not a cold war text, something that clearly should not surprise us, but will disappoint us if we demand blind fidelity to the source.

I am making no claims that the interest the film version of *Bewitched* holds is a direct function of the artistry of its creators, Nora Ephron, Nicole Kidman, and the rest. But neither would I make a similar claim as to the artistic talents of William Asher or Sol Saks. Ephron and Asher are certainly competent image-makers and I am appreciative of their efforts in making texts out of material of which I am quite fond. However, the purpose of cultural criticism is to reveal the ways in which textual artifacts engage their social contexts. The television show *Bewitched* is an extremely important, multiply-voiced document of mainstream America's response to the 1960s. I do not make the same claim for the film as a document of the early twenty-first century, but the film is nonetheless important as a testament to the persistence of the original *Bewitched*.

I have attempted to analyze the cultural response to that turbulent decade through *Bewitched* using the best critical methods. When I claim that the film version also participates in that analysis of the original show, I do not mean to equate a popular film with academic work. Instead, I observe that my intensive approach to the television show thrives on a love for *Bewitched*'s many wonders, a love that the makers of the much-maligned film also share. Academic analysis of television might learn something from the film's intensive cataloguing of *Bewitched* episodes, as it is in the multiplicity of television's narratives wherein lies the little box's greatest cultural contribution.

1. While episode guides—which I consider a remarkably intriguing form of literature—are readily available online at http://www.epguides.com, I relied instead on Herbie Pilato's *Bewitched Book* for episode titles and airdates. A fan of the show, Pilato has written an invaluable resource. While his prose is exquisitely, and annoyingly, adulatory of every facet of the show, the care with which he has written about it—relying on interviews with the cast and crew—puts to shame any previous academic work on *Bewitched.* I believe the solution is for television studies scholars to begin writing "academic episode guides," in which capsule reviews of each episode are not devoted to brief plot summaries, but instead to their thematic and ideological importance. While the short monographs in the "TV Milestones" series are not the place to accomplish such a feat, I believe this goal is an important one for the future of academic television studies.

2. For more on the importance of Mike Dann in television history, see Mitchell E. Shapiro's entry in Newcomb, ed., *Encyclopedia of Television.*

3. Much of *Bewitched*'s enormous success in syndication was the result of local UHF stations running the show in the early morning or late afternoon when kids were going to, or returning home from, school. Indeed, I did my entire Advanced Placement American history homework in high school while tuned to *Gilligan's*

Island, Bewitched, and other 1960s "vast wasteland" sitcoms. (I got a score of 5 out of 5 on the exam, so maybe it was not such a wasteland after all!)

The fact that I am now an academic media studies critic who writes about history is a karmic delight to someone whose parents, faithful adherents to the Puritan work ethic, were constantly telling him that watching TV while doing homework was wasteful. In any event, while *Bewitched* was a show that almost immediately appealed to children, its very recent status as one of Nick at Nite's prime-time shows—often on late at night after the children have gone to bed—indicates that part of *Bewitched*'s appeal continues to be for adults, even if in the nostalgic mode. As I write, *Bewitched* again airs in the mornings, at 7:30 on the West Coast (this time on the TV Land cable network), presumably constructing another generation of fans, watching as they eat their cereal before school.

4. The ratings information cited here is gleaned from Brooks and Marsh, *Complete Directory of Prime Time Network TV Shows:* "Prime Time Schedule: 1964–1971" (906–13) and "Top-Rated Programs by Season" (968–70).

5. By modernist, here and throughout this book, I refer to the artistic movement, as represented by Bertolt Brecht's *The Threepenny Opera* (1928), which responded to classicism by using a stylistically aggressive idiom to critique the status quo.

6. The best study of the rise of the television documentary in the wake of Minnow's speech is *Redeeming the Wasteland: Television Documentary and Cold War Politics* by Michael Curtin.

7. Jacob Smith provides a much-needed evaluation of the relationship between television's address of liveness and the laugh track in his excellent article, "The Frenzy of the Audible."

8. Steve Cox, author of an episode guide for *I Dream of Jeannie,* had the unusual good sense for a populist writer to include an essay on the show by the analytical Douglas, titled "Feminism and the Jeannie."

9. In 1998, Nick at Nite purchased the rights to all of the *Bewitched* episodes, and now TV Land also airs the (beautifully restored) color episodes. These restorations are now being released, season by season, on DVD, in both their original black-and-white and colorized versions.

WORKS CITED

Altman, Rick. "Television/Sound." *Studies in Entertainment: Critical Approaches to Mass Culture.* Ed. Tania Modleski. Bloomington: Indiana UP, 1986. 39–54.

Amory, Cleveland. "*Bewitched* [review]." *TV Guide,* October 24, 1964. A-54.

Andrew, Dudley. *Film in the Aura of Art.* Princeton: Princeton UP, 1984.

Asimov, Isaac. "Husbands, Beware!" *TV Guide,* March 22–28, 1969. 7–10.

Atkinson, Michael. "Oh, the Nora, the Nora: Every Little Thing She Does Is Tragic." *Village Voice,* June 21, 2004.

Barker, David. "Television Production Techniques as Communication." *Television: The Critical View.* Ed. Horace Newcomb. 6th ed. New York: Oxford UP, 2000. 169–82.

Boozer, Jack. *Career Movies: American Business and the Success Mystique.* Austin: U of Texas P, 2002.

Brooks, Tim, and Earle Marsh. *The Complete Directory to Prime Time Network and Cable TV Shows, 1946–Present.* 6th ed. New York: Ballantine, 1995.

Carr, Steven Alan. "On the Edge of Tastelessness: CBS, the Smothers Brothers and the Struggle for Control." *Cinema Journal* 31.4 (1992): 3–24.

Corber, Robert. *In the Name of National Security: Hitchcock, Homophobia, and the Political Construction of Gender in Postwar America.*

Durham: Duke UP, 1993.

Curtin, Michael. *Redeeming the Wasteland: Television Documentary and Cold War Politics.* New Brunswick: Rutgers UP, 1995.

Daly, Mary. *Gyn/Ecology: The Metaethics of Radical Feminism.* Boston: Beacon P, 1990.

Doty, Alexander. "The Cabinet of Lucy Ricardo: Lucille Ball's Star Image." *Cinema Journal* 29.4 (1990): 3–22.

———. "I Love *Laverne and Shirley.*" *Making Things Perfectly Queer: Interpreting Mass Culture.* Minneapolis: U of Minnesota P, 1993. 39–62.

Douglas, Susan J. "Feminism and the Jeannie." *Dreaming of Jeannie: TV's Prime Time in a Bottle.* Lead author Steve Cox. New York: St. Martin's, 2000.

———. "Genies and Witches." *Where the Girls Are: Growing Up Female with the Mass Media.* New York: Times Books, 1994. 123–275.

Ebert, Roger. "*Bewitched* (film review)." *Chicago Sun-Times,* June 24, 2005. http://rogerebert.suntimes.com/apps/pbcs.dll/article?AID=/20050623/REVIEWS/50524004/1023&template=printart. August 19, 2006.

Friedan, Betty. "Television and the Feminine Mystique." *TV Guide: The First 25 Years.* Ed. Jay S. Harris. New York: Simon, 1978. 93–98.

Hamamoto, Darrell Y. *Nervous Laughter.* Westport, CT: Praeger, 1989.

Heller, Dana. *Family Plots: The De-Oedipalization of Popular Culture.* Philadelphia: U of Pennsylvania P, 1995.

Himmelstein, Hal. *Television Myth and the American Mind.* 2nd ed. Westport, CT: Praeger, 1994.

Jones, Gerald. *Honey, I'm Home!: Sit-Coms and Selling the American Dream.* New York: Grove Weidenfeld, 1992.

Lane, Bill. "*Bewitched:* Sounds of the Harp." http://www.harpiesbizarre.com/soundfxharp.htm. July 30, 2006.

Lane, Christina. "*Bewitched.*" *Encyclopedia of Television.* Ed. Horace Newcomb. Vol. 1. Chicago: Fitzroy Dearborn, 1997. 180–82.

Lipsitz, George. "The Meaning of Memory: Family, Class, and Ethnicity in Early Network Television Programs." *Private Screenings: Television and the Female Consumer.* Ed. Lynn Spigel and Denise Mann. Minneapolis: U of Minnesota P, 1992.

Marc, David. *Comic Visions: Television Comedy and American Culture.* New York: Routledge, 1989.

McCarthy, Anna. "'Must See' Queer TV: History and Serial Form in *Ellen.*" *Quality Popular Television: Cult TV, the Industry and Fans.*

Ed. Mark Jancovich and James Lyons. London: BFI, 2003. 88–102.

Mellencamp, Patricia. "Situation Comedy, Feminism, and Freud: Discourses of Gracie and Lucy." *Studies in Entertainment: Critical Approaches to Mass Culture.* Bloomington: Indiana UP, 1986. 80–95.

Minnow, Newton. "The Vast Wasteland." *Equal Time: The Private Broadcaster and the Public Interest.* Ed. Lawrence Laurent. New York: Atheneum, 1964. 45–69.

Moss, Sylvia. "The New Comedy." *Television Quarterly* 4 (Winter 1965): 42–45.

Newcomb, Horace, ed. *Encyclopedia of Television.* Chicago: Fitzroy Dearborn, 1997.

———. "*Magnum:* The Champagne of TV?" *Channels* (May–June 1985): 23–26.

Pilato, Herbie J. *The Bewitched Book: The Cosmic Companion to TV's Most Magical Supernatural Situation Comedy.* New York: Delta, 1992.

Putterman, Barry. *On Television and Comedy.* Jefferson, NC: McFarland, 1995.

Rowe, Kathleen. *The Unruly Woman: Gender and the Genres of Laughter.* Austin: U of Texas P, 1995.

Schatz, Thomas. "*St. Elsewhere* and the Evolution of the Ensemble Series." *Television: The Critical View.* Ed. Horace Newcomb. 4th ed. New York: Oxford UP, 1987. 85–100.

Searle, Ronald. "Wherein a Dastardly Plot Is Uncovered." *TV Guide,* June 18, 1966. 15–18.

Shapiro, Mitchell E. "Dann, Michael." *Encyclopedia of Television.* 2nd ed. Ed. Horace Newcomb. Vol. 2. New York: Fitzroy Dearborn, 2004. 655–56.

Smith, Jacob. "The Frenzy of the Audible: Pleasure, Authenticity, and Recorded Laughter." *Television and New Media* 6.1 (2005): 23–47.

Spigel, Lynn. "From Domestic Space to Outer Space." *Close Encounters: Film, Feminism, and Science Fiction.* Ed. Constance Penley et al. Minneapolis: U of Minnesota P, 1991. 205–35.

Taylor, Ella. "Television as Family: The Episodic Series, 1946–1969." *Prime-Time Families: Television Culture in Postwar America.* Berkeley: U of California P, 1989. 17–41.

Viviano, Francis P. *Video and American Values: A History of the Television Program as Ideological Metaphor, 1947–1978.* Diss. U of Michigan, 1978.

White, Mimi. "Crossing Wavelengths: The Diegetic and Referential Imaginary of American Commercial Television." *Cinema Journal*

25.2 (1986): 51–64.

White, Patricia. *unInvited: Classical Hollywood Cinema and Lesbian Representability.* Bloomington: Indiana UP, 1999.

Williams, Raymond. *Television: Technology and Cultural Form.* London: Fontana, 1974.

Willis, Sharon. "The Politics of Disappointment: Todd Haynes Rewrites Douglas Sirk." *Camera Obscura* 54 (2003): 131–75.

Zinn, Howard. *Post-War America: 1945–1971.* Indianapolis: Bobbs-Merrill, 1973.